MASTERING THE NYMPH

MASTERING
THE NYMPH

GORDON FRASER

BLANDFORD PRESS

POOLE · NEW YORK · SYDNEY

Series editor: Jonathan Grimwood

First published in the UK 1987 by Blandford Press,
Link House, West Street, Poole, Dorset BH15 1LL

Distributed in the United States by
Sterling Publishing Co., Inc.,
2 Park Avenue, New York, NY 10016

Distributed in Australia by
Capricorn Link (Australia) Pty Ltd,
PO Box 665, Lane Cove, NSW 2066

British Library Cataloguing in Publication Data

Fraser, Gordon
  Mastering the nymph.
  1. Trout fishing   2. Fly fishing
  I. Title
  799.1'755   SH687

ISBN 0 7137 1741 6

Typeset by Word Perfect 99 Ltd, Bournemouth, Dorset.

Printed and bound in Great Britain by
Biddles Ltd, Guildford and King's Lynn

CONTENTS

1 · WHY MASTER
THE NYMPH?

As we'll see in the section on tackle, early in my angling career I had to survive the incredible set-back of 16 blanks on the trot. In a sense, this did me a favour, as I was ready to check out any possibility of improving my results. At the end of the 16 trips, I hooked and landed a trout.

On gutting the fish at home in the sink, it was full of what I then thought were brown beetles, and I now know were *corixa*. They bore no resemblance to the lures and wet flies that I'd been fishing so far. If this was what trout wanted to eat, I reasoned, this must be what I should fish. It all seems so simple and logical now, but then the techniques weren't so common, and only a handful of anglers had mastered them. I rapidly became obsessed with the trout's diet – something that I heartily recommend to every reader of this book. I read a few magazine articles and library books to guide me. But my main guide was what I saw in my spoon or guttings.

I tried to copy everything, from the largest caddis right down to the tiny red mite, a creature not dissimilar to its terrestrial counterpart, and about the size of a 26 hook! (Needless to say, the tiny pattern didn't work too well, and though you'll often spoon these bright red specks from a trout, it's a better idea to compromise with a non-specific red fly like my longshank Seal's Fur.)

The natural progression of my attempts to copy insects was that I went into the close-copy school, always trying to produce what *I* thought was a really close copy of the trout's food. I rapidly discovered that my ideas didn't correspond with the trout's. I don't know much about art, but if there's a style of painting known as realistic, I'm now in the style you'd call impressionist. There are some exceptions where I've gone some way towards the natural insect, such as the *corixa*, or hatching sedge.

Let's briefly develop that theme. No one could run down the excellent close-copy patterns of someone like Bob Carnill, the brilliant Nottingham fly dressing authority, whose special buzzers look ready to crawl from the box. Bob feels that on hard days, a close-copy can make all the difference. But for more than 90 per cent of the time, my impressionistic patterns (and Bob's) are completely adequate.

However, there is room for experimentation. My BP (blended fur and polypropylene) range of nymphs is an attempt to improve one aspect of nymph imitation. When viewed closely nymphs are not simply one colour, but are blended from various shades. My blend of stippled hare fur, and seal, helps to build an impressionistic picture giving that effect.

Having studied the appearance of the insect, I proceeded to read up on its behaviour and life-cycle. That gave me more and more clues as to how to fish my flies. It also helped to free me from some prejudices. I found out that, though the main sedge hatches seem to abound in the high summer months, the cased larva of some sedges, the caddis, is about throughout the year.

So why fish the imitative way? For me, it was the solution to my strong desire to take regular good catches of fish. As it turned out there was more to it than just that. I found that the fish I took were often better than other anglers', and that I sometimes took fish when others failed. I also found that it was a most satisfying thing to deceive – rather than attract or lure a fish.

There are two parts to that statement. It's not just about using a fly that looks a little like the trout's food that counts, but also adopting the correct retrieve – as we'll see in the next chapter. Any fly can be made into an attractor or lure in the right (or wrong) circumstances. Fish any fly fast, and a trout may come tearing after it and grab it. The fact remains that this will more often be a stockfish that hasn't yet got wise to the idea that jet-propelled underwater objects are best not investigated by closing the mouth over them. But to deceive a fish which has settled into a natural feeding pattern, the presentation must be perfect. We can slightly exaggerate some factors, like the size of the fly, or speed of retrieve; but overall, to deceive a trout, we've got to give a pretty good impression of nature.

All this is fine in principle, until we consider one significant factor. Trout are, in my opinion, not unlike humans in their feeding habits. Far from being like cows that chew all day, trout are predators who grab a meal when it's handy. They don't feed all the time; and while they can be easy to catch when gorging on a heavy hatch of fly – if you've got the right imitation handy – they do occasionally need something like a lure pulled through them to stir up their interest in hooking themselves on the end.

Sometimes when trout do feed steadily for long periods, it's down to a lure or a non-specific imitator to catch them – as when the fish cruise, mouths open, through the daphnia soup that appears in good quantities on most reservoirs during the summer. The plankton soup is impossible to imitate, but something pink or orange often does the trick.

It's in quality fish, however, that the nymph fisherman collects most of his wages. Picture your average stockfish: he goes into a fishery with dozens of similar fish, and, with few exceptions, 70 per cent of his fellow stockies are harvested in the first few weeks. The rainbow especially, but also the brown trout stockie, is a shoal fish. Cruising around with his rapidly disappearing mates, he must see quite a few lures and flies of every sort whizzing past his nose. He may even be lucky enough to lose a fatal race with another fish for the fly.

But despite the fact that trout have pretty daft eating habits, they do in time learn. Some evidence suggests that they get wise to the colour of a lure pretty quickly. Indeed it's often the case in the early season that the dedicated lure fisherman must change his fly colour after every fish or so if he wants consistent success.

If the stockfish escapes those harrowing first few weeks he will discover natural food, and join in some of the feeding patterns of resident fish. He will eat small fish and daphnia, but, mostly, nymphs. By this time, his tail will be growing back, and he'll have taken on that blue silver sheen that makes the rainbow the handsomest of fish. His flesh, too, will be a healthy pink, not dyed by artificial pellets, and when cooked he'll once more taste

A super bag of nymph-caught rainbows that support Gordon's idea that the nymph sorts out better fish.

like nature intended. He'll be altogether a smarter fish, and though his enforced fast may mean that he's not yet a good deal heavier than when he was stocked, he's well worth catching.

Smarter, yes – but not necessarily harder to catch. In a really prolific hatch of say, buzzers, he'll be in there pigging with the rest of the fish. His attitude is to grab it while it's hot, and before those yobbo stockies get here. And then, if your skill and your flies combine, he may be yours.

Of course, there are ways of catching more fish. You can make a special note of stocking days at your local water, buy a season ticket, and be sure always to pop in on Tuesday mornings, or whatever the day. Then your quickly-pulled Black Lures, Tadpoles, or Pink Panthers will slaughter fish almost every time. But where's the real pleasure in the sport, when it becomes merely a chancy form of pick-your-own?

For me, nowhere. On the other six days of the week my nymphs will continue to take better and, sometimes, more fish: fish that have been fooled by the nymphs I'm offering, tied by me, and fished to deceive. That will do for me.

11

2 · TACKLE

The fly fisherman is lucky: he doesn't need to hump the piles of tackle of the committed coarse fisherman along the banks. Seats, umbrellas, and keepnets are all out of the question. He must be light, mobile, and free of anything that will spoil his casting. So why, I wonder, does it still take me and a boat partner ten minutes to get from car to water?

The answer is that the modern boat angler feels undressed without any of the various weapons that he might possibly need, far away from the hoard of tackle in his car. But these days the nymph angler, with one light rod, a floating line, and a box of flies can be as free as a bird if he likes. Wandering along the banks of a green and pleasant reservoir, pitching a fly here and there as the mood takes him, can be the most pleasant way of enjoying our sport. However, even if there is only a small amount of essential tackle, it must be carefully chosen.

The first problem for the nymph angler is that no doubt as a novice he will catch more fish, especially in the early season, by lure stripping, so he may well come to the more delicate side of the sport ill-equipped, not knowing at the start exactly what he'll need.

Don't get me wrong – not only is there a place for big rods and heavy lines in nymphing, but some very competent anglers never use anything else. They don't feel that their presentation suffers by the use of weight-forward 8 floaters, or even heavier shooting-heads. That sort of tackle lets them cast a long way and cover fish the average nymph man won't. But for me, and probably the vast majority of nymph fishermen, lighter tackle is the thing. Indeed there's a new trend in stillwater trouting for some very delicate tackle indeed: lines as light as AFTM (American Federation of Tackle Manufacturers) 4, and 3lb leaders. In difficult conditions, such tackle can be a revelation, as what seemed impossible fish suddenly become catchable. But in truth, this very light gear is really only practical in a boat, where it's usually easier to play fish in open water. For the all-round, or bank-only nymph angler, a slightly heavier approach is safer and far less nerve-wracking.

I came into the sport with a totally impractical cane rod, lent to me by a kind man who dragged me away from the coarse fishing world. He took me to Eye Brook where I experienced immediate success with a Peter Ross that I had lathered in grease and fished dry, letting the line drift out on a backwind. I took a rainbow, and thought that this game was easier than it really is. A second trip with him produced three more fish, and by now I was truly hooked. Sadly my tutor died just before Christmas of that year – we'd fished the last weekends of the season. I carried on the following year with the same technique, without his advice, and managed just 11 fish all season. At one stage I had 16 blanks on the trot! In June and July I stood surrounded by chaps catching fish while my efforts produced nothing.

After the cane rod, I got hold of the first of many glass rods, and by the advent of carbon rods, I'd settled on a style of rod I liked. Middle- to tip-actioned, it could pick up line quickly, either to cast to moving fish, or to lift into a pull. It was a cheap Shakespeare rod, onto which I'd fitted Fuji rings, and I used two of these quite happily. I ignored the high-priced early carbons, which seemed floppy to me, and often broke during casting.

It was not until my entry into the trade, and the opportunity to try and to reject several carbon blanks, that I was hooked on carbon rods. The blank I chose was not the most expensive; indeed it was in the medium price range of the company that sold it, and still is. For me it had, and has, all the virtues of the old glass rods, and the added advantage of extra strength, enough stiffness, and extreme lightness compared to glass. For heavier work – punching a lead-preg into a wind – I use its 10 foot big brother.

The blank I chose was 9 feet 6 inches long, and rated AFTM 6 to 8.

(The big rod casts lines of AFTM 8 to 9.) It will punch out 20 yards of fly line with ease, and pick it up, slack and all, swiftly enough to set the hook.

Of course such a stiff rod is better at long range, and I can see an argument for a through-actioned rod when nymphing small fisheries. Here, you may have only feet, not yards, of line and leader beyond the tip ring. A through-action rod will absorb fishy bounces far more easily than a stiffer tip-actioned weapon. But at longer range, there's a lot of stretch in both plastic flylines, and long leaders, to absorb the sudden jerks of a fighting fish. That said, with light leaders below, say, 4lb breaking strain, a tip-action rod can lead to some nasty snap-offs even on the take. It's really very rare indeed for me to fish a lighter point than 5lb. If I do though, especially on one of my more powerful rods, I'll incorporate a 6 to 8 inch piece of powergum into my butt section of leader. This acts as an efficient shock absorber.

Fittings on rods are more a matter of individual choice. I do strongly recommend building up or turning down the rod handle until it's really comfortable, or it may affect your casting. I like a reel seat that pushes the reel up the handle, and close to my hand. That seems to balance better to me, despite what you might hear to the contrary. Light single-leg modern silicon carbide rings, Japanese or British are superb, very long-lasting, and neither affect the action of the rod through adding too much weight and stiffness, nor allow the line to slap too badly against the blank – slowing down your casting. When whipping these on, do make a few turns above the ring to hold it firmly in place. To be honest though, I whip and superglue my rings on, these days.

There's a very strong argument for matt-finished rods: rod flash really does scare fish. Watch the rods signalling on any bright day on a reservoir. However, I only varnish the whipping on my rods; modern carbon blanks have a pleasant satin gloss already. Rather than rub that down – possibly damaging the rod – I opt for laziness, and let the algae, and water-borne silt gradually build up on the rod, wiping them down maybe once a season. Believe it or not, this actually helps.

FLY LINE CHOICE

Eighty per cent of my fishing is done with a floating line, and probably three quarters of my floating line work – all of it on the big waters – is done with a forward-taper line. I can cast these further and they are to some extent easier for a fish to straighten out when it takes. It still has a belly of line to move, but behind it, a thinner running line is a more sensitive bite indicator than the thick belly of a floater.

At short range on a smaller water, the double-taper allows more sensitive presentation, and is less likely to scare fish.

Actual line size depends on conditions. I can chuck an 8 line further than a 6, but I know my presentation will not be so delicate. Still, there are other factors to take into account, especially if you're on a tight budget. In a season I can wear out two quite good-quality forward-tapers, as they tend to crack where the thick belly joins the more flexible running line. A double-taper cracks less easily, and will always be easily reversed if it does, allowing you to use the other end. As to price, I stick with middle-of-the-range lines, which won't break my heart if they quickly deteriorate. For the novice, I see nothing wrong in using a carefully chosen Mill-End. These are less-than-perfect reject lines, usually from the better manufacturers who are really concerned about quality, and are available from several sources at very low prices.

Colour of fly line is a vexed question in these days of fluorescent green, orange and yellow floaters. Some claim that anything but a jet-black line scares fish. Others make a claim for white – after all, what colour is a sea gull? I compromise by going for pale colours, green, grey and beige, that I can see quite well without fluorescence to help me. I'm not one of these nymphers who claims to see the tip of a fly line move 2 inches 20 yards away. But I do like to see the line, both to watch for it straightening, and for fishy movement in the water near it.

Personally, I don't object if the tip of the line slightly sinks through the surface film. (In fact on some occasions I actually encourage this. After rubbing the leader down with mud, I'll also rub down the first couple of feet or so of the line tip.) This helps to get the leader under too, and if I want a high float, I get out a pot of grease, and make it float. Thus most of my well-used floaters are actually slight sink-tips. As I've said in the chapter on techniques, I also use a standard shop-bought sink-tip a fair bit. Although many anglers find these awkward to cast, I find that their usefulness far outweighs any problems with casting.

A full sinker, whether described as intermediate sinking, or slow-sinking, keeps on going down until you pull it upwards. As most of my 'fishing calls for very slow retrieves, I would never be able to fish at the depth I wanted for long enough to do me much good.

There are two exceptions. One is the use just occasionally of a slow-sinker in a flat calm to avoid the tell-tale signs of line wake. Even then I need an unnaturally fast retrieve to keep the flies up in the water. The other is the use of a very fast-sinking line to fish the Booby series flies hard on the bottom. I favour lead-impregnated lines – or 'lead-pregs', as most anglers call them. These go down very quickly and are a little more flexible than those that sport a fine lead core.

REEL CHOICE

Lines are loaded onto a reel. You can pay a fortune for a reel these days, and whatever you buy will last a lifetime. But the same is true of many of the cheaper reels. For years I've used a well-known cheap single-action reel, and never had a problem, or felt the need for anything more sophisticated. About the only time I'll play a fish off the reel is when I hook one winding in – which is not so uncommon as you might think.

NYLON

It's mostly a matter of personal choice which nylon you use. If you find one you like, that knots reliably, and isn't given to mysterious breakages, then stick with it.

Some nylons are a little stiff, others lack stretch, or are too stretchy. For some years now I've used the same brand, which was available in clear, sorrel, and – my favourite when I could get it – green.

The availability of various shades of nylon has set me thinking over the last few years. Water in trout fisheries tends to be clear, or tinged green or brown. There's no reason why the angler shouldn't carry the same brand of nylon in several shades, to cover all eventualities.

Try to buy fresh nylon. It's a pity it isn't all date-stamped, really. Keep it in a cool dark place: sunlight and heat speed up its deterioration as does water. On the other hand, I have some spools of nylon that must be eight years old. Kept in a cool dark cupboard, they are still used with confidence. Some of my customers now buy nylon from me in bulk, and providing they store it sensibly, it can be a good investment against ever-

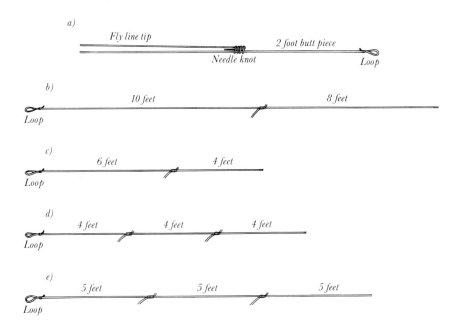

Fig 1

Leader make-up – taper the nylon down if you require, stage by stage, but it makes little difference in leader turnover

rising prices. But leave it in your car, and you're asking for trouble.

If fish shy away from your nylon you can always go down a size. On the other hand it may be glare – some nylons are very glossy. In that case, a gentle rub with scouring powder will remove the gloss.

LEADERS

Of course, nylon is made up into the vital link between fly line and fly, the leader. I attach a stiff butt piece of 11 lb nylon and loop on a leader to that. My overall leader length is rarely less than 15 feet. Depending on conditions, I always used to use 4 lb, 6 lb or 8 lb. It's probably symptomatic of some slightly more difficult fishing these days, that I often find myself using a compromise 5 lb point. A fishing friend has reported

17

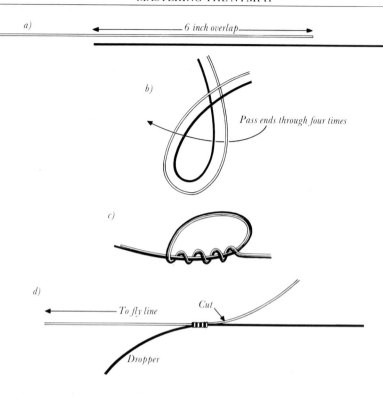

a) 6 inch overlap

b) Pass ends through four times

c)

d) To fly line — Cut

Dropper

Fig 2

The Cove or Water Knot is Gordon's choice for joining nylon together

a similar phenomenon. Really we're conning ourselves to think that the extra pound's strength makes any difference; it's all about confidence in your tackle and tactics, as we'll see later.

When adding a dropper (virtually never more than one), I use the well known Cove or Water knot. In recent seasons controversy has raged about which end of the knot should be left on to form a dropper after the two lengths are joined. I still favour the end that points back up the leader towards the rod. Droppers should never be less, or a lot more, than 4 inches. I try to ring the changes with my point fly while leaving a reliable pattern on the dropper. This is a great help in not shortening the dropper too quickly by nipping off and tying on a new fly too often.

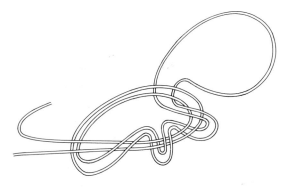

Fig 3

Triple Overhand Loop

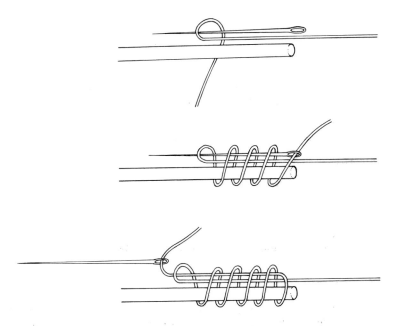

Fig 4

Needle Knot

19

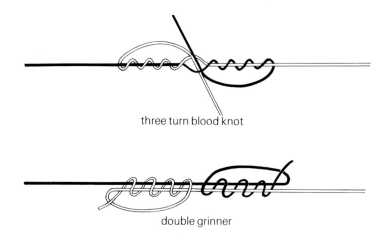

three turn blood knot

double grinner

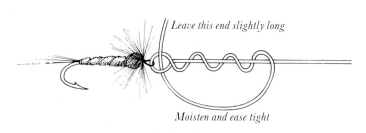

Leave this end slightly long

Moisten and ease tight

Fig 5

The Blood Knot – Gordon prefers to leave a 'tag' rather than tuck this knot

Incidentally, don't try joining two nylons of widely different strength (or, more to the point, diameter), as they tend to work against each other and break easily.

All knots should be clipped off as neatly and tightly as possible, to minimise wake when the flies are retrieved.

FLIES

We'll list a lot of flies and how to dress them later on. But not everyone wants to tie flies, and quite a few, thank goodness, want to buy them. (Which is just as well for one-man 'pro' flydressers like myself!)

Of course, I'd highly recommend using a good flydresser, and there are quite a few around. A good test when ordering, is to order several flies of one size and pattern, and line them up side by side. They should all be consistent in appearance like peas in a pod.

But there's more than that to it. My early flies were monstrosities: fat and uneven. The nymph man has to demand higher standards, and proportions are all-important. Buzzers and olives are skinny little nymphs, and dressings should reflect this, with slim abdomens and neat blob-like thoraces. *Corixa* are tiny creatures, not the thickened fattened blobs often sold. Sedges are a bit plumper, but even then, I have little faith in great thick wadges of dubbing wound onto the hook.

A great many imitative patterns are overdressed to my eye, and the greatest offenders are the overseas flies, often tied by native workers who've not the remotest idea what they're imitating – or failing to imitate. As we'll mention in a moment, the marrow spoon is *your* guide.

Another thing to check when tying on any fly, is that it looks the right colour when wet. There's little point in choosing exactly the primrose yellow of a spooned sedge pupa, only to find that the fly has a black silk underbody that ensures that when wet, it looks darker. It happens more than you'd think, especially with floss-bodied flies.

Big bulky nymphs do have a place, often as a compromise between the nymph and the lure: stocked trout like nothing better than to thump into an overgrown Mayfly Nymph, or one of the modern creations in bright colours that, though called nymphs, look like nothing natural that ever swam. Heavily-leaded flies of this sort are sometimes very successful when stalking a big suspicious trout – or a big freshly stocked one!

SUNDRIES

The nymph angler really does need to carry a floating agent, usually some sort of grease, and an agent to make his leader sink. While there are commercial versions of both, and I usually use Mucilin®, one of the

In goes the spoon. This one-off stock rainbow had little of interest in it to help Gordon on a hard day.

best-known greases, there are a number of household substitutes in most kitchens and bathrooms. In the past I've even used lard!

Don't apply grease in blobs, or lumps. Apply it smoothly and sparingly. Moreover, don't use it unless you have to. There are alternatives like Suspender Buzzers, and Booby Nymphs which will float of their own accord. Adding grease to the line pushes it into the surface film, ensuring that it's more visible; and as you would imagine, the leader makes a considerable wake in the water when it floats high. Even when dry fly fishing, the fly will float of its own accord without any kind of floatant quite well – and if it sinks into the surface film, and doesn't float on it – well, that's the kind of presentation I prefer, as you'll see later.

Sinking agents are available commercially, too, but almost everyone I know uses a nasty concoction of their own. Mine's a bit of yellow garden clay thoroughly mixed with detergent and sealed in a mini-grip bag to keep it moist and malleable. If you're on the bank you can usually find a suitable lump of mud. But my little lump of soil goes with me everywhere – especially in the boat.

PRIESTS AND SPOONS

We have enough trouble (and more coming, I fear) with people opposing our sport without giving them further cause for complaint when we kill a fish. While it's not necessary to carry a perfectly balanced hand-crafted stag's horn priest, every trout angler who intends to kill fish, should carry a suitably hefty and solid 'bonker' which can be used to strike the trout a firm blow behind the eyes, and kill it very quickly. Having killed his trout, the good nymph angler will take the chance to use a spoon to test the stomach contents. After all we're in the business of copying and imitating the trout's diet.

The spoon is a long thin scoop. It should be slid gently but firmly, down into the trout's stomach, given one twist only, and withdrawn slowly and carefully. It's often handy to have a small dish or something similar into which to tip the contents.

LANDING NETS

There are some silly little tennis racquet-sized nets around, described as being for trout. Avoid them like the plague. Instead get hold of a good sized net, for instance, a triangular net with 20 inch arms, and a reasonable handle, of at least 4 feet long.

Don't strain any net. Once the fish is safely in it, slide it up the bank; don't attempt a straight lift. If the fish is very large, get hold of the net frame before lifting the whole thing out. These two precautions should ensure a long life for the net.

As a matter of interest, where the bank is fairly smooth and snag free, I prefer, like quite a few experienced anglers, to beach fish. This is done by playing out the fish, and carefully sliding it, head up, up the bank. It's

23

Rod Woolnough nets Gordon's prime 4lb rainbow. But he should grab the net itself – look at the bend in the handle.

not a stunt to try with a too-fresh fish. But when you've mastered it, it can be safer than netting fish.

LINE TRAYS

If there's one item of tackle that almost deserves a chapter on its own, it's this one. I've often said, I'd rather leave my net at home than forget my line tray.

Years ago I was knee deep in the Grafham margins. It was back in the days when 3 lb fish were common, and I was fishing a Black Lure on a sinking line, when I had a steady draw, lifted and the line started to rapidly disappear towards the middle of the reservoir. Then with a jerk,

Gordon swears that he won't forget his net again, as a 2½lb brown rolls in the marginal weed. Note the loose loop from the line tray – allowing free movement of the casting arm.

everything went slack, and I cursed before looking down and finding my line firmly wrapped around an old tree root. With a line tray this wouldn't have happened, and a good fish would probably have ended up on the bank.

Line trays are usually linked with shooting-head equipment. They generally consist of a square tray worn by the left hip, about 6 inches deep. As line is retrieved it's dropped into the tray. That process, of course, keeps it clear of the bankside, and the water. With fine shooting-head backing this is especially important, but with any line, bankside obstructions are a problem. Away from the bank you might imagine there'd be no problem. But a sinking line does just that – it sinks. Obstructions like that Grafham root under the water can obstruct the line, so can weed, and you can end up standing on it. Just lifting it up out of the water to cast can be a problem when it's sunk, and your optimum distance will certainly be harder to achieve.

And with a floating line? Well, imagine the effect of a side wind blowing the retrieved line away down the reservoir. Even if it doesn't snag-up on something, to pull all the drifted line back, and up, is a trying task. Loose floating loops of line can get tangled in each other. You might not notice until forced to give line on a racing fish. But when a loop through loop knot jams in the butt ring, it's too late to do anything about it. (As we'll see when we talk about techniques, that sort of cross-wind can be the very best for the nymph angler as it swings round his flies most naturally.)

You may see pictures of American anglers overcoming this problem with loops of fly line trapped in their mouths while they cast – looks painful to me. You might think too, that you'd be safe on the smooth stones of a dam like that at Grafham or Eye Brook. But even here you can walk on the line easily, or find sharp edges on apparently smooth flagstones.

Rougher dams like Rutland make the tray more essential than ever. I've even seen an angler moving along the dam there after landing a fish, dragging loose line. It got hung up, and with one swift jerk he found he'd snapped it clean in half and converted it to a shooting head. Sharp stones can slice through plastic fly lines at will.

Where space permits, I do like to wander along the bank, without having to wind up any loose line. With my fly line coiled in a line tray, this leaves me free to cast at any fish I see moving.

26

A good line tray will be roomy, light, and fold up easily for transport. On the bank you'll see every version from baby's paddling pools to other floating structures made of net stretched over an old inner tube. But I still prefer the strap-on sort.

On some smaller waters where I'm not likely to cast far, and therefore won't have a lot of line loose between butt ring and reel, I don't always use one. But without a line tray, on a big water, I feel undressed when I'm on the bank. If it might seem like a luxury item, I justify my use of it by the thought that in protecting my line from the bankside sand and grit abrasion, and in better fishing efficiency and therefore more fish, a line tray pays for itself in a season.

3 · TACTICS – IT'S NOT WHAT YOU FISH, IT'S THE WAY YOU FISH IT

'WHAT DID YOU CATCH IT ON?'

That must be the commonest question in trout fishing. But nine times out of ten the question should be not *what,* but *how* did you catch it? In my opinion some 60 per cent of nymphing success revolves around tactics and techniques. Which fly you use comes next, and last, but perhaps most important, comes confidence in what you're doing, and the fly you're fishing.

So how to get this confidence? I suggest working your way through the various methods I'm going to outline, and making the most of any success that comes your way. There are good days and bad, but with patience and observation the bad days should become less common, and the successes more frequent. Then, just as you think you've got it all worked out, the trout will prove you wrong. This of course is the attraction. If I thought I could catch fish every time I went I'd soon get bored and have to go in search of something more exciting, like free-fall parachuting.

But let's get down to catching a trout on nymph.

WHEN THE WIND BLOWS

When planning a day by the water it pays huge dividends to keep an eye on the wind for several days before the trip. This applies mainly to the large stillwaters – and remember, get it wrong at somewhere like

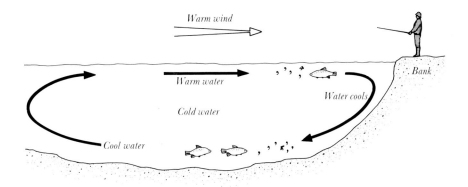

Warm wind

Warm water

Cold water

Cool water

Water cools

Bank

Fig 6

Fish into warm winds in spring – they concentrate fish on the windward shore

Rutland, which has a perimeter of about 22 miles, and it's an hour-and-a-half's wasted journey.

In the early season on the bigger waters, it takes quite some time for the water temperature to rise to the optimum for the trout to feed. Factors other than the weather should be taken into account. The comparatively shallow Eye Brook or Blagdon will warm up far faster than Rutland Water, for instance.

Generally the warmer water will collect on the side of the reservoir the wind is blowing to. Add to this the fact that an onshore wind will be stirring up the early season trout food – sluggish caddis, perhaps *corixa*, bloodworm and the like, even earthworms over flooded land – and providing the colour of the water isn't too mucky, that's where the fish will be. In fact that's a golden rule for the nymph angler: fish are lazy creatures and you'll find them where the food is, and where they can expend the minimum energy to get hold of it.

On meeting the windward shore, the water then goes back into an undertow, and meets cooler deeper water. Thus the only exception to the general early season rule is when a very cold wind has been pushing cooler water across the top of the reservoir, and cooling the best feeding areas. Then, trout are just as likely to be on the lee shore. Of course, as we'll

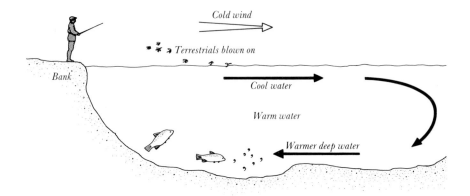

Fig 7

If the wind is cooler than the water in spring, get it on your back. Warm water, food and fish gather on the lee shore

discuss later, punching a line into a head wind is not for the average caster, and those without the muscles of a Mr Universe. So, very often in the early season I choose to go afloat.

BOATS – MOBILE CASTING PLATFORMS

To me, 90 per cent of the time – in fact nearly all the time when nymphing – a boat is just a casting platform.

As the Bristol anglers are showing us more and more, a drifting broadside-on technique – loch style, traditional, over the front, call it what you will – can be used very effectively to fish nymphs. Often they cast to moving fish, and on many occasions the drift is very slow. Combining that forward movement with slow pulls, means that a very nymph-like retrieve is possible. In fact, fishing a team of nymphs with a palmered fly on the top dropper is an underused and deadly method. So bear all that in mind for balmier days when the surface fishing is at its height.

For much of the rest of the season, an anchor, or even two, one at each end of the boat, is a vital part of your equipment. It's worth having your own, with an extra long rope, as those supplied on most reservoirs aren't much good. So let's head for that rough shore and anchor around 60 yards off, looking for water no more than 15 feet deep, ideally 6 to 10 feet.

Little bays seem to shelter the fish, and if you fished the water the season before, try to remember the location of the thick weedbeds. These are now rotting on the bottom, and providing food and shelter to a lot of early season bugs.

Take time when you get there to anchor the boat just where you want it, to get yourself organised, net to hand, and to stop panting and puffing. Use this time to have a look around, as even on a cool day there may be the odd fish rising. The most likely food form to bring the fish up is tiny dark buzzers, but there's also the chance of terrestrials or the odd early pond olive. A splashy rise at this stage of the season suggests that the fish has taken either an adult buzzer just trying to get off the water, or a terrestrial, most likely a beetle at this time of the year. Humping swirls, or a slight flattening of the water, indicate fish taking hatching pupae. Probably you'll see precisely nothing. But let's assume that the odd fish is showing.

SURFACE NYMPHING TECHNIQUE

Set up a floating line, using the longest leader you can easily handle. With the wind behind you this can be quite long. A 20 foot leader is my choice with a dropper 8 feet up from the point. I nearly always fish one or two flies. One reason is that I like to fish them as far apart as possible, with the flies working individually and not as a team. Of course, it's impractical to fish three flies 8 feet apart, as you need an incredibly long leader, and even then you'd not get a fish within netting range before the top fly stuck in the tip ring.

We'll talk about the various fly patterns later in more detail, but a typical cast for this time of the year would be a 12 or 14 Buzzer on point or dropper and a similar size Fraser Nymph on the dropper or point. Good buzzer colours are black, brown, dark olive or on some waters, claret.

The last touch is to rub down the leader with a proprietary sinker, or better, and cheaper, a carefully chosen, slightly gritty lump of mud – which of course you must take out with you. Choose carefully: some blue mud at Rutland actually seems to make nylon float. As with virtually every method, I start with careful short casts with the minimum of splash before gradually lengthening line. Cast around in an arc, covering all the angles. Sluggish spring fish may not move too far for food. As soon as the flies land, start a smooth figure-of-eight retrieve. The mud will take them smoothly through the surface film, and the dropper will fish about 3 inches down with the point 6 to 9 inches deeper.

If you catch a fish, try to do exactly whatever brought you the take again. That's easier said than done, but remembering what you did after finally netting the fish, can lead to another very quickly. 'Sequencing' as it's called, is very important. Don't pause after catching a fish, as they don't always feed for long. Get straight back in and get another. If you don't get a fish, keep casting to the maximum distance, but give the flies a little longer to sink before retrieving them.

DEEPER NYMPHING

If you don't pick up a fish, keep your casting distance at your *comfortable* limit, and gradually allow the nymphs more time to sink until eventually you find the correct feeding depth, or you feel that fishing consistently deep is taking too long. After a while you may pick up bottom debris that fouls your cast and flies, and stops you fishing effectively. Either way, this is the time to switch to a leaded pattern that will get down quicker. It will also be easier to judge the depth it's fishing at.

Among my favourite early season patterns are the Eye Brook Caddis, and the leaded Hare's Ear. The first copies the cased larva of the sedge. The second is a good general grubbing pattern, not unlike the Alder larva, another available trout food in the early season, and quite a good caddis pattern too.

Even then, in very deep water on the edge of effective nymphing – 10 feet or more – it's time to get out the sink-tip line.

SINK-TIP SESSIONS

From a boat, most of my early season nymphing is done with a sink-tip line. It will have a sinking section of various lengths according to make, built-in to the end of a floater. For some anglers this makes the line unbalanced and difficult to cast: I don't find this problem too bad. Some lines have very fast sinking tips and possibly this accentuates the problem. I use lines with medium sinking tips and don't seem to encounter problems that make me want to leave them alone.

Even with medium sinking tips we must allow some sinking time for the line tip and flies – up to a minute in 15 feet of water. Even then, retrieving will make the flies lift slightly. There's nothing to stop you using leaded flies on a sink-tip, but one advantage is its better presentation – you can use unleaded patterns and still fish them deep.

Ideal patterns are red based-bloodworms like my simple Buzzer Larva, or my longshank red Seal's Fur Nymph. Too many fishermen have got the idea that buzzers can only be fished in the surface; any of the patterns we've mentioned will also catch when fished deep. The buzzer larva lives mostly in the mud, coming out only occasionally when disturbed, and is nearly always found near the bottom. Its pupa, the next stage, can be around at all levels for some time before hatching – a process that takes place at the surface.

Years ago I fished on the first day of a week's holiday. It was at Eye Brook back in the days when I worked for British Steel, and we got budget priced season tickets.

It was far from an ideal day, with that often fatal east wind, and a bright clear sky. The weekend sport had apparently been tough with only a few fish taken on deep-sunk lures. But I'm always an optimist (to start with, anyway), and I tackled up at the car with a sink-tip and a Cove Nymph on the tip, and a Black Spider on the dropper.

I rowed away from the lodge and decided to try Sam's Dyke, which the wind had been blowing into for several days. I tried every fly in the box and a variety of retrieves, while I was anchored about 60 yards out. Not a touch. I moved down towards the Cowshed where the odd fish had come out the day before. I was feeling a bit chilled by the wind but the short row warmed me up and restored my confidence.

However, as I passed the big bay just behind the point of the Island, I remembered that after being choc-a-bloc with weed all summer, it wouldn't have been fished much since last season. So I decided on a pause, and a few casts here. I picked a spot slap in the middle of the bay (known as the Pens), and settled down to fish. By now I had a Black Buzzer on the point and a Cove on the dropper. After about 20 minutes at last, a take, a long smooth draw that was impossible to miss. Shortly

33

after, I boated a brown of about 1 lb 4 oz. Nothing else happened for about half an hour, and I wondered if it was a one-off. I decided to spoon the fish. By now I'd decided the fish hadn't really been feeding and had taken the fly as it might have snatched at a lure. But to my surprise it was full of bloodworms. They were half an inch long, and many were still alive.

In those days I used a simple pattern – an even simpler pattern – with only a basic wind of red wool round the hook. I popped one on the point. Even now I had a 20 minute wait before anything happened. I had turfed out the fly and left everything while I had a coffee. Then the rod started jumping about of its own accord. I made a grab for it, and over went the tip as I played out a good brown of 2 lb with the fly deep in its throat. It, too, was full of bloodworm.

After this hefty hint, I tried a dead slow retrieve. The point fly began to pick up weed and debris, which obviously decreased its attractiveness. On went another red pattern on the dropper, and the same slow retrieve produced another thumping brown. The dropper was fishing just clear of the bottom debris, the point fly bumping bottom. A retrieve as slow as a single figure-of-eight every few seconds was essential.

I finished the day with 12 browns, the best weighing 2 lb 10 oz. Having discovered the secret I went back on Tuesday and Wednesday, and got 9 fish, and 14 respectively.

Over the three days the only angler who took the trouble to ask me *how* I was fishing, not just what, came and anchored beside me in the same area, and took eight fish. Few other anglers managed anything like that over three days.

SLOW RETRIEVES

Let's pause here and consider what we do when we pull that line back. Most right-handed anglers will hold the rod pointing more or less right down the line, with just a very slight loose 'swingtip' of line onto the water. The right index finger is lightly trapping the line, or forming a sort of extra rod ring.

The left hand does the retrieving. The simplest way is to pull line back in pulls of between a few inches and several feet. But for a smooth retrieve we need the good old figure-of-eight. In this, the left hand gathers the line,

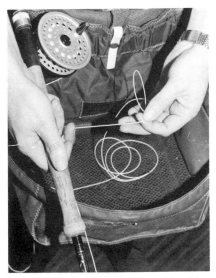

Gordon's personalised figure-of-eight. Line pinched between finger and thumb.

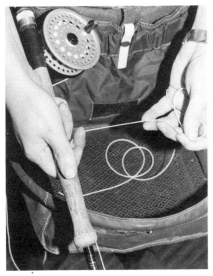

The line is wrapped around the fingers.

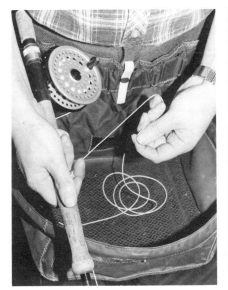

The rest of the fingers gather the line into the palm.

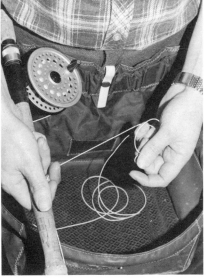

The thumb and finger open to grab more line – the line held in the palm is dropped into the line tray, and the process is repeated.

wrapping it around the fingers before dropping it – in my case into the line tray. This movement means that you can get a steady retrieve without breaks in the movement of the flies. You can do this as slowly as you like – or with practice, quite fast.

CRUISING FISH CAPERS

In the warmer days of May and June the rainbows will be cruising, often right over open water. In these months you can sometimes just anchor and with a floating line fish the flies over quite deep water. All you need to do is wait for a shoal to come by and cast to any fish that show. At other times fish will appear from nowhere.

Algae can build up in many waters by July or August, and this can be a bonus as it masks a lot of the bright sunshine, and encourages the fish to continue moving higher in the water. A thick green soup of daphnia can have the same effect, although these microscopic organisms tend to sink, away from bright sun. It's often thought that daphnia time means large gaudy lures like my Pink Panther or the Whisky Fly. However, don't neglect standard nymph tactics with a longshank orange Seal's Fur, or a Zulu Nymph, as these are just as deadly – even though the fish will only have the green soup of daphnia in them when spooned, and perhaps a few small buzzers.

TOP WATER TACTICS

Through the warmer months you'll often meet with occasions when the flies must be right in the surface film to score, certainly in the top few inches. This is often the case at dusk in an evening rise, but it can happen during the day too, when large numbers of hatching flies are trapped on, or near the surface. Lightly greasing the leader is one solution, but as soon as you start to move a greased-up leader, in all but a good rolling chop, it will leave a wake that will put fish off.

A useful alternative is to incorporate a buoyant fly into your cast. I use a leader with two droppers, one 5 feet from the point, and another 5 feet further up. The point could be a Suspender Buzzer, or one of my Booby Nymphs (of which more later), or as the season progresses into fry time (or at any time that there's fry about), an Ethafoam Doll. (On the droppers two nymphs – most often Buzzers, or two more Suspender Buzzers.) A very slow retrieve, allowing the flies to drift on the wind, and staying in touch, is all that's needed. The fry pattern in particular is very visible, and will act like a bite indicator. Cast this outfit near weedbeds, and the fry itself may be taken.

WHEN TO SPEED UP

When anglers tell me that they can't catch on nymphs I always tell them to slow down the retrieve. There are exceptions though: fast retrieves score with olives, and with hatching sedges. I've seen sedges positively racing to the surface to hatch. Another fast mover, as we'll see, is the *corixa*. Mix the retrieves up from very fast, to hardly moving. But it's amazing how often a dead drift on the wind will take fish, when pulling won't. As we'll see later, the *corixa* calls for a set of rather unusual retrieves, not the least of which is the sink-and-draw.

BACK ON THE BANK

Most anglers associate nymph fishing with the bank, and it's here that the majority of nymph fishermen will spend most of their time. From late April onwards, until mid to late June, and after the end of August, results on the bank will often beat fishing on a boat. For the rest of the season, you may well have to fish in the early mornings and late evenings to get results. One exception is the Eye Brook where any kind of sport enjoyed during the day often ceases in the evening. An exception, perhaps, that proves the rule.

EXTRA BANK TACTICS

Most, if not all of the tactics outlined for boat fishing will also work on the bank. Of course, the floater is your main weapon, except where there's deep water close to the bank, and a sink-tip can be necessary.

GONE WITH THE WIND?

Bank fishermen, even more than the boat angler, should remember the wind. I've lost count of the number of times that the typical row of bank anglers, all with their backs to the wind, and looking for easy casting, catch perhaps one fish, while the hardy souls that brave the difficult casting into the wind, catch quite a few more.

In the early season the place to head for is the rough shore. Now's the time to shorten the leader, and I go down to 10 or 12 feet, with a dropper about 4 feet from the point. A leaded pattern on the point can help everything to turn over. Don't overdo the lead though, as a heavy weight whistling past your ear in a face wind is a dangerous thing – for the same reason, wear a hat and sunglasses to protect head and eyes.

The lead is also a help in keeping your flies reasonably deep. Your

Fig 8

Productive spring bank fishing spots

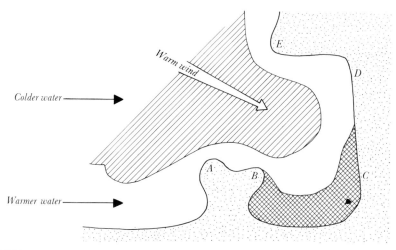

///// *Deep water*

▧ *Coloured water*

A. *Right-hander can cover deeps close in and swing line over shallows*

B. *Best spot: right-hander can reach deep water, fish extensive shallows with a drifting line, and reach productive edge of coloured water*

C. *Right or left-hander can punch out line against wind to reach edge of coloured water – fish move close inshore*

D. *Hard but good fishing for right-hander – easier for left-hander*

E. *Left-hander has easy casting and fair fishing*

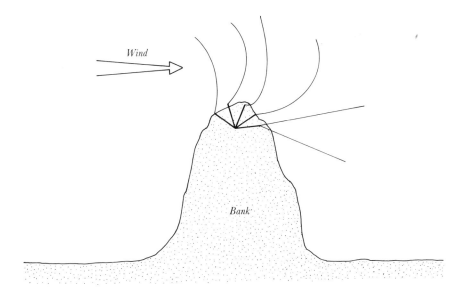

Fig 9

Right hander fishing a point. Cast across the wind and let it swing. Try also longer straight casts down the wind

retrieve with a floating line is mostly governed by the speed of the waves coming towards you. Avoid spots where the water is very dirty, as more often than not this will put fish off – though the edge of a dirty slick can be a productive area.

If the wind is too strong to cast into, or the water is dirty too far out to cast past it, we obviously must look for a bank spot where we can get the wind on our side – the left side for a right-handed angler. Points on the edges of bays are typical spots. From such positions it's possible to cast across the wind, and drift flies round on the side wind into the bays.

A dam can also be productive. It's not often that there's much mud at the bottom of a dam, and consequently there's less likely to be colour in the water as the waves roll onto the stonework. Indeed, the undertow will drag a lot of surface food down, and fish will sit in the depths awaiting the feast. On concrete bowls, of course, you rarely get coloured water problems, but on the other hand, you don't have all the interesting bays

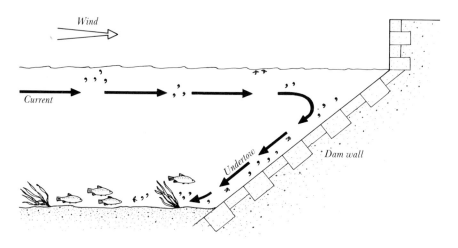

Fig 10

The effect of a wind onto any bank – the undertow drags down surface food

and points that you have on a more natural reservoir. On some days you'll find it more productive to cast along the dam rather than straight out from it. Often the fish will come close in looking for food that can have been swept the length of the reservoir before being pushed down the wall by the undertow. One of my customers fishes a corner of the dam at Rutland regularly, as a season ticket holder. Perfect conditions for him are a chop coming straight at him. He then casts along the dam, fishing just 6 to 8 feet from the stones. I think he takes more 3 lb-plus fish in a season than any other angler I know.

Once the water is generally warmer, we can start to enjoy our sport in greater comfort. Again headlands or points are among the best spots for ambushing shoals of fish as they move in and out of the bays, or along the shore. We can also often cover the slightly deeper water that can hold fish during the brighter part of the day. Again, one of the deadliest methods on a point is to swing the floating line and the flies around on the wind, letting them almost fish themselves. Slowly-moved flies seem to bring steady takes at this time.

From time to time it may be necessary to 'mend' line. Lift the rod, and flick the belly of the line in the direction of the drift. Keeping that tight

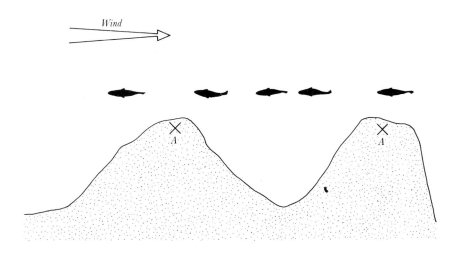

Fig 11

Trout moving upwind often cut across the ends of bays, not entering. Fish at position A

bow in the line prevents your flies from being dragged unnaturally fast by the wind. Follow the line round with the rod, but don't try to lift up into those confident draws. Instead tighten sideways into the fish.

The slow wind movement of the line calls for a different balance of flies to make sure that they're fishing at the right depth. It's surprising how a floating line will move unleaded flies up high in the water as it drifts slowly. But even then a buoyant fly on the cast may be necessary to keep the whole cast high in the water. On the other hand, you can add some grease to the leader more safely under these conditions, as a drifting line will make less wake.

WEED OR FISH?

As the water warms in the spring you may often come across mats of rotting weed rising vertically in the water and hitting the surface with a distinct dimple that is easily taken for a rise. This is one time when the bloodworm can suddenly find himself high in the water. I remember one evening at Rutland when my son and I spent a frustrating evening fishing all manner of flies between beds of floating weed, where fish were often seen to be rising. Only later did we discover that anyone who for some unknown reason had caught on, and fished a bloodworm close to the surface, had caught fish.

Other nymphs too, suddenly find their weedy shelters rising to the top, and drop out, making a feast for the cruising trout.

Years ago I first encountered this phenomenon at the Eye Brook. What apparently happens is that the rotting weed produces gas, and at the right temperature this expands enough to float the weed to the surface. On that Sunday I had slept in late and missed out on all the best spots. I ended up in Sam's Dyke. As I arrived, I met two chaps just leaving who said there were rising fish everywhere in Sam's, but that they couldn't touch them. When I got to the water's edge there, sure enough, were a couple of rising fish about 20 yards out.

The water was between 3 and 5 feet deep, and I tackled up with a floating line, and a long leader with two nymphs. It's always a good idea not to scare feeding fish before you've even cast to them. Fish feeding close in are easily scared when a line lands in their heads, so do as I did that day, and gradually lengthen your cast to cover the water. At the same time, I mixed up my retrieves for speed and depth. I must have cast to dozens of what I thought were fish in the next hour.

While I paused for a cast to sink, I noticed a fish-like swirl within a few yards of my casting position. It looked exactly like a trout taking a nymph. A few seconds later it happened again, and this time I was able to pick up what was in fact rising weed for a closer look.

By this time I was almost convinced that there were no trout in the area. But the mat of weed was full of food. At first I noticed just a couple of bloodworms, but breaking the weed up I found several more, and quite a few of the green buzzer larvae you also encounter. (In fact, though the bright red bloodworm is the best known of the buzzer larvae, they also appear in this green, and in greeny brown mixtures of both colours.)

I decided to join the two anglers who'd already left, but as I walked back to the bank I trailed my line behind me, and suddenly had a savage take. The resulting fish was a 1 ½ lb brown which had taken a Black Spider on the dropper. In went the spoon . . . the fish had quite a few blood red larvae, and hundreds of minute green ones in it.

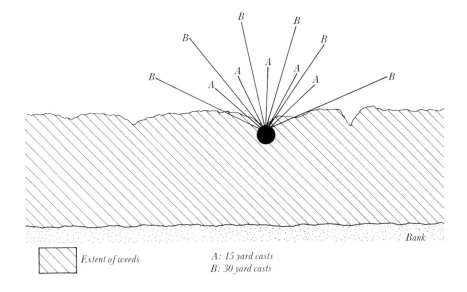

Extent of weeds

A: 15 yard casts
B: 30 yard casts

Fig 12

Stay back from the edge of the weeds – using marginal weed as a screen – and start with short easy casts, before reaching out for fish

I was without a bloodworm pattern, and was reduced to clipping down a couple of Red Palmers from the box, and cutting the seal's fur body to make it slimmer. The problem was how to fish the flies. I reckoned the trout were taking the larvae as they dropped vertically from the weed. I decided to allow plenty of sinking time, then to fish dead slow.

Nothing happened on the first couple of casts. On the third there was a gentle take on the drop, which I missed. A few casts later I hooked a take on the drop, and landed a brown trout of similar size to the first. I ended the day with five nice browns all around the 1 ½ lb mark. All the takes came on the drop, and perhaps not surprisingly, I missed about a dozen more. There wasn't a touch while retrieving. The trout were totally preoccupied with picking up the falling larvae.

Faced with this situation nowadays, I let the flies sink, then whizz back the line ready to recast. This is probably the only occasion when I actually try to see the tip of the line move – it will appear to be disappearing down

43

a hole, and often the pull seems to be unmissable. Sadly, I miss a lot, as they're some of the most difficult to hit. Don't forget that the feeding pattern can change, so keep mixing in the odd slow retrieve between casts.

Of course, there are other sorts of weed that can bother the bank angler, and often it can seem so thick that it might be impossible to fish. But the nymph angler should never ignore weed as it shelters a great deal of food in the shape of larvae, nymphs and fry, and quite a few fish, too. Some of these will be grown-on early-season stockies that have settled into a natural feeding pattern and are improving in weight and condition – apart from anything else, they'll have been little troubled by the sink-line lure merchants here. So don't be tempted to abandon weedy areas as the season progresses: fish them if it's humanly possible. A floating line and small flies will keep foul-ups to a minimum.

Eventually of course, without the aid of weed-cutting boats, some areas of your favourite water may become unfishable – mainly because, with the best will in the world, you can't pull a trout through 5 yards of weed. But by using only one fly you can eliminate the chance of your dropper getting caught up. In some circumstances your nylon will slice through weed like a cheese cutter. And sensible use of grease on the line and leader will hold your flies clear of the weed. Often, in the clearest looking areas, you'll find weed just sub-surface.

There are holes in every patch of weed, and at the height of summer, many of these underwater caves and canyons will shelter trout. Here they're protected from the brightness of the sun's rays, and can feed to their heart's delight.

We have to tease the trout out of the weed, and I use one fly on a very long leader, greased to within a couple of feet of the point. After casting towards the holes, I either try a fast figure-of-eight, or a series of fastish short strips to draw the trout's attention, and hopefully get him to quickly make up his mind and come up and grab the fly. When this works, takes can be very positive indeed, and are often accompanied by a swirl on the water's surface as the fish rolls quickly onto the fly. But don't strike at this movement: wait until you feel the fish. One solution seems to be to hold the rod a little higher than usual, and wait for the slight bow in the line to go solid. Keep on the move, fishing the holes with a few casts, then trying the next. We're looking for residents – not cruising fish, and if they're not at home, or not interested we're just wasting time.

At this time of the year the best patterns are likely to be a Hatching Sedge, Corixa, olive patterns, or a more general fly like the Fraser Nymph.

DAMP DRIES?

There are occasions when the surface of the lake must look like flypaper to a fish looking up from below. Trapped hatching nymphs, drowned egg-laying adults, or adults that have damaged themselves emerging from the nymphal shuck, are all glued in the surface film, struggling slightly maybe, but just drifting slowly until a hungry trout ends their suffering.

This is the time for Damp Dries. More about these later, but fishing techniques for the flies are simplicity itself. Just pitch one out, and leave it to drift. Watch for takes, but you'll often find with these flies that fish simply swim off with them, straightening the line with an unmissable take. If you think about it, it's obvious: no moving flashing nylon, and no wake to frighten a trout. The natural insect couldn't escape. If the trout wants it he takes it in a leisurely fashion. The take to the artificial insect can reflect this. Don't strike at the takes – lift smoothly. The Damp Dry is also ideal for fishing the weed holes. Pitch it in and let it sit. Tighten firmly after lifting into the fish – don't let him back in the weed.

Another time to adopt this method is a flat calm when fish are rising. Pitch out the fly and do nothing. A nymph would need retrieving, and however slow, a huge tell-tale wake would go out from the line. A Damp Dry sits glued in the film – fishing for you.

Of course dry fly doesn't come within the scope of this book. But to clarify this, we're not talking here about the fully-fledged adult, high and dry on the surface. No, we're talking about that swamped, just sub-surface creature, a hatching nymph, stranded and stuck, damaged in its shuck. You'll often spot these creatures drifting past, making a sad sight with their mortal struggles to free themselves. My Damp Dries with their large soft hackles bunched in two neat groups are a handy imitation, and fishing them in a normal nymphing situation is no more difficult than the static methods we've discussed.

Tie on a couple, in varying colour shades, lightly grease the leader, and the wings of the fly. Now squeeze the fly between finger and thumb to bunch the wings in two. The body of the fly will sink slightly, with the wings in the surface film. Now just cast out and let the flies drift in the normal cross-wind way (or out on a backwind). Spectacular results can come on the rough shore as trout look for an accumulation of wind-driven victims.

DYING WEED IS FRYING WEED

As the weedbeds die back (something that seems to happen earlier in a warm summer than in a cold one), we can get back into areas that we have ignored since they weeded up.

Coarse fish fry, and *corixa* seek the shelter of the dying weed; trout follow. Late olives often appear. At the Eye Brook these are smaller and paler than the spring variety. The buzzers keep going right through to the winter. So it's often a Corixa on the point, and though, as we'll see, *corixa* tactics aren't like those for other nymphs, a Black Spider, ginger Hackled Pheasant Tail, or Fraser Nymph on a dropper will take its share too.

SMALL WATER TACTICS

The vast majority of reservoir tactics kill from time to time on the small waters. Indeed on some muddy holes, the fishing can be so easy, that you'll be able to run through a whole list of tactics in one day, and catch fish after fish.

I find the clear water small fisheries more interesting. I class waters of under 20 acres as small, and 20 to 100 as medium. There are some fascinating waters in all classes. But when it comes to the very small ones, the stalking waters, where you can spot and cast to your fish are the only ones that hold my interest. Wading is rarely necessary, and there's usually deep water close in. Fish the flies right in if you're just casting at random. It's amazing how often these purpose-dug fisheries have a gully right at the edge – often full of better and crafty fish that can't swim out of range on the small pool – so they hide under the bank. One of my fishing friends literally trod on a 10 lb-plus rainbow when he got too close to the undercut weedy edge at Avington.

More interesting is to stalk the individual fish, Often this is the only way to ensure a full day's sport on the best well-stocked fisheries, where random casting often gets a quick, easy, and costly limit. Instead, with a floater, a 10 to 12 foot leader (a short leader to aid accuracy and get the fly on the fish's nose), and the ever-essential polaroid sunglasses, wander the banks looking for fish of better proportions. Anglers who have this off to an art – like Bill Sibbons – tie flies specially for the job. For myself, my leaded green Seal's Fur Nymph is my number one choice. I concentrate on the 10 feet of water out from the bank, scanning the depths all the time. Fish spotting is an art. Look for grey shadows, flashes of silver, things moving where they shouldn't, and tell-tale torpedoes lying motionless. It's an art that can take a long time to master, and some anglers never do – but it's all part of watercraft, and essential for regular success. Use the available cover – rushes, weedbeds, small bushes – or, when you spot a fish, stay well back from the edge.

It can work to cast to a fish with an audible plop. But sometimes this will scare him. At this casting range your presentation should be perfect, and usually it must be, for success.

Try to drop the nymph near the fish's head. He may take it on the drop. He may even take it if you hold it motionless before his nose. But most likely he'll take it as you lift it, in the classic style. The lift you employ is similar to the end of a loch-style cast. Start by retrieving line with the hand. As you reach the full extent of the line, lift the rod slowly and smoothly up too. You can even dibble the nymph on the top.

Who knows what manoeuvre may tempt a suspicious trout? If he follows the fly don't stop, don't speed up. If you do, he'll often have it, but more often than not, the steady retrieve arouses the least suspicion.

He may of course cock a fishy eyelid at the fly (I know they don't have them, but you'll almost see him wink), smile to himself, and belt off to the other end of the pool forthwith.

Next time, if there is one, try something small, but still weighty enough to get down quickly. My Shrimp or Corixa patterns are ideal. Men who make an art of this method, like Bill Sibbons, replace the thorax of Buzzer or Pheasant Tail with a lead shot, which you can still get on his nose quite quickly. He'll have seen far fewer small leaded patterns, and eaten several tiny nymphs to every large damsel or mayfly nymph. All in all the small fly is less suspicious to him. But there's a problem. We don't start with a small nymph, as we often can't see when it's taken. The art is to watch for the tell-tale 'wink in the water' of the trout's white inner mouth. When it disappears you instantly set the hook. Hard fishing, yes, but fascinating.

47

Often you may find space a little restricted, but you'll still get in in the bushy tree-lined areas. No one fishes these. The trout know that too, and often the better fish, just as they do in rivers, hang out in these tough spots. How then, to get a line out here, with a tree over your head, and a bush on either side?

The bow and arrow, slingshot, or as I call it catapult, cast is the solution, if the fish are fairly close in. Often you can't even swing the line out in such spots. So grab hold of the nymph in one hand, and the rod in the other. Poke the rod through the hole (slowly – flashing rod varnish scares more fish than anything I know). The shortish leader is eased through the tip ring, followed by a little fly line. Pinch the fly by the bend between finger and thumb and point the rod at the trout. Pull back on the leader to flex the rod, then let go of the nymph, but be very careful with this method not to hook yourself. With a bit of luck you'll get the fly out far enough to hook a fish. But you'll need 8 lb nylon to hold a good one in the confined space, and a net with a good long handle.

All this is fun, but I still can't really take small waters seriously. They respond quickly and awkwardly to every change of weather, and the fish rarely have time to start any kind of natural feeding, before they're out on the bank. After all, no area is out of casting range, and the fish sees flies all day and every day. For this reason, I do find that the larger nymphs, presented with an unnaturally fast retrieve, are usually successful. On the whole, it's all a bit too easy for my liking. Just before writing this book I came across one notable exception, however: a lightly-fished syndicate water to the east of my home. Run by John Hamilton, everything seems to be just about perfect on his very rich water. John's policy is to stock just once in early spring. His members are true fishermen, not fishmongers, and don't kill for killing's sake. Consequently by mid-summer the fishing is very difficult, but highly rewarding, and when fish are caught, they are truly superb, fattened on a natural diet, and genuinely able to match up to the standard of Grafham's or Rutland's finest.

DIVE BOMBING AND DEPTH CHARGING

So far we've only spoken about the tactics of fishing *down* from the *water's surface*. Recently it's become clear that fishing *up* from the *bottom* has its advantages too.

48

Gordon shows the right way to lift a netted fish. With this Avington rainbow safely in the net, his hand has slid down to take the weight off the telescopic extension.

The Booby series of flies are really basic nymphs with a little buoyancy added. They grew out of my experiments with foam beads, after a long chat with the editor, at that time, of *Trout Fisherman*, John Wilshaw. We had discussed using the Suspender Buzzer, with its stocking-enclosed foam bead, and had also considered extending it to other patterns like a Hare's Ear.

To cut a long story (which we'll tell elsewhere) short, we ended up with a series of lures and nymphs with foam beads in pairs at the head. This made them float, and gave them action in two ways: one by pushing water at the surface; and two, by creating a turbulence which, particularly on the Booby Lure patterns, made the body and tail materials swirl and wiggle under the water. Fishing techniques for these patterns are all a matter of speed, length of leader and buoyancy. Say, for example, we start with a *3 foot* knotless leader: no knots to pick up weed, and only 3 feet to keep the fly down where we want it. The line is a lead-preg fast sinker.

Cast out and let the line settle on the bottom. When it has, the fly is 3 feet up. Easing the line back brings it down; stopping makes it rise like a hatching nymph. A slow stop, start, retrieve ensures you don't snag the bottom. A longer leader and a faster retrieve will have the same effect.

This gives us an alternative tactic in a head wind onto a dam. As we said, the fish sit at the bottom of the dam, and nose into the undertow sucking in food. By casting out the line into the head wind, you'll find you can gradually slide your fly and line down the dam wall into the undertow. Let out line, and hold on. Watch the line for takes. This virtual swingtipping tactic, the fly wobbling nicely on the undertow, can be deadly, and beats the hell out of fighting a savage wind any day.

DETECTING THE TAKE

Great nymph anglers are sometimes seen as gurus, their less perceptive disciples grouped at their wader-clad knees, all seeking the secret of one thing – detecting the take of a biting trout.

How nice it would be to simply say, 'nothing to it'. Well sometimes there isn't. Good draws, and solid pulls, swirls on the surface, even sub-surface flashes of silver are all reliable tell-tales, but unfortunately they're rare. Many new recruits tell me that they've fished for hours with no sign of a take. During that time though, they've probably touched a great many fish, but felt nothing.

The hard pulls come when a trout turns away with the fly, and sets off in another direction; or they come when you're pulling a Sedge or Corixa quite fast. But on a dead drift, or when the flies are just inched back, with, inevitably, some slack somewhere between hand and fly, what to look for? A take can feel like a touch on the weeds or another snag. Lift and feel for a fish firmly. Don't worry about it being a false alarm – you've lost nothing.

The inevitable slack can be put to good use too. Watch the in-and-out curves in your floating fly line for straightening. Or watch the 'swing tip' of loose line from tip ring to water. Don't strain your eyes trying to watch the fly line tip – watch the fly line as near to it as is comfortable. On shorter casts, by all means watch the line tip, but don't let it distract you from the more easily spotted movements if your line straightens. A pull of the line away from you will be harder to spot than sideways movements like the line straightening.

As you improve, and if you fish regularly, you'll begin to 'feel' takes. I agree with other anglers that it almost becomes a form of ESP. You feel a fish, and react before the mind has time to say, 'Don't be ridiculous.' It's not ridiculous when there's a fish on the end!

Your reaction could be entirely mental, it could be the eyes spotting something the thinking brain doesn't take in, or it could be a subtle change in the line pressure on the finger that the mind, not the skin, feels. Whatever it is, both I, and many other anglers, have often lifted into fish without knowing why. There's been no physical or visual reason. And if there is the slight physical or visual indication, my golden rule is, if anything out of the ordinary happens, tighten into that, too!

But before I set up as Maharishi Gordon in a Melton Mowbray trout fishing commune for psychic nymph anglers, let me issue a warning: none of this comes without regular fishing. You very easily lose the 'feel' for fishy mouthings at your fly. Over the last couple of years, I've fished a little less – and I've noticed the 'feel' slipping away.

4 · THE BUZZER – THE STILLWATER NYMPH ANGLER'S STANDBY

What the stillwater angler calls the buzzer, and the entomologist calls the *chironomus*, must be the most common trout food nationwide. Almost any lake at almost any time will have a hatch of some member of this family, and, once the insect reaches the larval stage, it's constantly on the menu for hungry trout.

The stages of the life cycle that are of interest to the angler are manifold. The larva, best known by the name bloodworm (although not always that famous blood red colour by any means, as we've already noted in the chapter on tactics), gives way to a pupal stage which seems to cover most of the colours of the rainbow. To imitate all of the buzzer pupae you're likely to find you'd need a suitcase of flies. Fortunately you can get away with less, as we'll see.

Finally, the adult, whose distinctive hum gives the insect its angler's name. How many buzzer pupae actually make a safe journey to the surface, and split their shucks before taking off, I don't know. What I do know is that trapped adult buzzers, struggling to slip free of the pupal shuck, are a regular sight on the waters I fish, and an easy meal for the trout.

HABITAT AND BEHAVIOUR

The larva, which from now on we'll call bloodworm, spends much of its

Fig 13

Buzzer (Chironomus) *pupa*

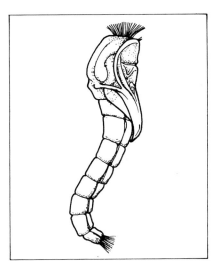

Fig 14

Buzzer (Chironomus) *larva, or bloodworm*

existence in the bottom silt, in thick weedbeds and in algae. In its most recognisable form, the bloodworm appears to be simply a tiny red worm, and though close up you can see that its pattern is more complicated than that, it lends itself to the simplest of imitations. It's virtually impossible to simulate the bloodworm's lashing, wriggling swimming action with a fly, though attempts with rubber bands and marabou have worked well. But for myself, I see no reason to use a complicated pattern.

My simple seal's fur pattern, and my new plastic one, have been among my deadliest nymphs. Which begs a question: if this creature spends much of its existence buried, how do the fish find it? It must pop out, or be washed out sufficiently often for them to know all about it; and in its bright, almost fluorescent red form, it must be pretty distinctive. Certainly I regularly spoon bloodworm from trout.

Of course, as we've noted, there are occasions when bloodworms suddenly shift in large numbers up to the surface, generally in warm weather; and as we've also seen, they can get dragged out of cover by rising mats of dead weed and algae. All my nymph fishing experience leads me to believe that we don't fish red patterns often enough – it seems to be a deadly colour on many occasions.

Buzzer pupae are probably what anglers think of initially when the word nymphing comes into the conversation, and with good reason. Trout love to eat these freely available little wriggling beasties, and their lifestyle makes them a target, from the depths to the surface.

After pupating from the larvae, they emerge to swim, quite efficiently, in the lower layers of the lake. They also hang motionless and free drifting, something that does the angler a favour, as the many underwater currents can gather up the pupae and push them along in concentrations that will attract the trout. But it's the rise to the surface for hatching (eclosion), that makes the pupa susceptible to the trout. The insect whizzes to the surface, hangs there, tail down, then turns to lie horizontally as it emerges through the surface film. The skin becomes a shuck as the creature pumps in air, and takes on a silvery appearance (something that accounts for the success of many traditional patterns with tinsel bodies). Then the shuck splits, and the adult buzzer emerges.

Throughout this process, the insect is susceptible to any cruising trout. And hatches often seem to happen in ideal conditions for the angler – overcast with a nice ripple, the ripple making it easier for the pupae to burst through the surface tension. Hatches, too, usually involve literally thousands of pupae. The trout will rarely resist such a wonderful feeding opportunity. Of course, hatches also take place in a flat calm – which brings problems we'll discuss later.

Grubbing one of his plastic bloodworm patterns brought Gordon this fine small water rainbow – despite a threatening sun and flat calm conditions.

Pupae that don't make it make a sorry sight; a tangle of legs, adult body, translucent shuck, all glued immovably in the surface film. It must look quite delicious to a trout. The successful adult lets everything dry and inflate properly, and sits on the surface for a moment; a vulnerable stage. Within a day or two it's back on the water mating, and after laying eggs in the water, the spent female midge becomes another easy target. On occasions, too, cruising trout clean up the left over shucks of the hatched buzzers.

WHERE AND WHEN TO FISH

Although we do the majority of our nymphing in water up to 15 feet deep, it's difficult to recommend a typical buzzer pitch. I've seen them pop up over 100 feet of water at Rutland.

One thing to look for is the softer bottoms. The buzzer will be found far more often over a soft bottom, than over gravel or rock areas. There's nothing like a good hatch to get the swifts and martins down over the water, so keep an eye out for them, and hurry to the area.

As for when: the dawn and dusk periods often feature a good hatch, especially in warm weather, but this is one creature that will take advantage of warm overcast days to hatch during office hours. Which is a bonus for the angler who likes, or has, to fish all day. But, as we'll see, I have a suspicion that there are some pretty dramatic hatches through the night, when it is after all, safer for the buzzer to get clear.

SIZE AND COLOUR

There is no time throughout the whole year, when buzzers in one form or another, may not be on the trouty menu. They're the bread and potatoes of their diet. And, being so important, you'd expect most anglers to have a clear understanding of their lifestyle, and fishing technique. But they don't: so many fishermen think only of buzzer fishing in the surface film. As we'll see, that's far from the rule.

The red bloodworm is the best colour of larva to imitate, but can we narrow down the multi-coloured pupa to a few colours? In the past I've dressed every colour under the sun, and after seeing some blue/green larvae, I even tried bright blue pupa imitations with some success. But for

With three nice fish already in the bag, a sudden change of feeding pattern has sent Gordon back to the fly box.

practical fishing, I've narrowed the pattern and colours down to a handful: black, brown, olive, fawn, ginger, green, claret, and red should suffice as general patterns.

While it's difficult to go through the seasonal variations on your own water with any hope of accuracy, I can give you some rough guidelines that will apply anywhere when it comes to colour choice. Early season black, or perhaps more common, dark brown buzzers will be prevalent; paler shades follow as the water warms, so look for dark olive buzzers next, followed by pale browns and pale olives. By mid-summer things get hectic, and a spooned trout may contain a whole range of sizes and colours. Big fawn or buff buzzers appear, gingers and very light olives, along with a tiny lime green buzzer, which also appears in a dirty yellow shade. Bright bottle green buzzers arrive too, as do bright orange on some waters. As the season advances we return to darker colours.

Obviously I match the colour of my buzzers to the natural, and two slightly different patterns, the Cove Nymph, and the Fraser Nymph, are excellent imitations of dark brown, and fawn or buff buzzers respectively. But the whole question of buzzer pupa colours is interesting, to say the least, and it's always worth noting the local variations in your spoonings. Local that is, not just to specific waters, but often to a particular area of the water.

Back in the great Grafham days, before bank erosion and the lack of weed made bank fishing a waste of time at the once proud water, one of my favourite areas was Gaynes Cove. Right in the corner of the Cove there is a small ditch that used to carry discharge water from the nearby treatment plant. This water was loaded with a rusty orange brown sediment, which would cover the whole of the bottom of the bay for a couple of hundred yards around the mouth of the stream.

In this area, and nowhere else, you could find a really bright hot orange buzzer all through the season. But as you moved away along the bank, the colour seemed to gradually change back to the more common browns and olives, and fawn. And thereby hangs another tale, as those fawn buzzers brought about the genesis of the Fraser Nymph (see Chapter 16).

I've come across sandy coloured buzzers in newly flooded gravel pits, and an almost white buzzer in a newly flooded chalk pit. But as the bottom silts up under a coat of weed and algae, the buzzers revert to more normal colours. It seems that the buzzer adapts to the environment by changing its colour to match the bottom. Some experimenting here with a fish tank and different coloured sheets of card could be fascinating. After all, the buzzer viewed close-up is not one colour, but an amalgamation of colours which combine to give an overall impression.

It was close observation by Peter Gathercole, and his superb photography in *Trout Fisherman* magazine that made me look a little closer. I've already described how I came away from close-copy patterns, but the buzzer is one nymph where I've gone a little way back again.

The BP series now incorporates everything I want in a buzzer. 'B' is blended fur – a hare's ear and seal combination that gives me a stippled effect; 'P' is polypropylene – the ribbing material I use, which gives me translucence and the suggestion, perhaps, of an inflating shuck. Were I limited to three colours, they would be fiery brown, dark olive and black in that order.

I've already given you a few thoughts on the dressing of nymphs in Chapter 2. They're particularly relevant to the buzzer pupa and the first thing to consider is the size of hook.

As we saw at the start of this chapter, the natural *chironomus* is around in sizes varying from a few hundredths of an inch, to an inch or more, depending on sub-species. Add to this the complications of tiny almost identical 'Phantom' midge pupae (*Chaoborus*), and mosquito pupae where present, and a spooning may produce a bellyfull of minute creatures, seemingly only imitated by a size 20 hook, and even that will be too big. As even a gentle trout take can straighten out the strongest 20 hook ever made (that is if you ever get the point to stick in in the first place), I limit myself to 10s, 12s and 14s on the majority of occasions. Smaller is hard to dress, to say the least.

I do compromise by short-dressing the little Williams style Black Gnat on a 14 hook to imitate small black gnats and midges. But I've yet to find that I catch enough fish on tiny flies to make it worth the effort. Other anglers strongly disagree with me, especially in the USA, where they have a passion for tiny flies.

If larger hooks are my choice, however, I've no place at all for fat flies. I took this to such extremes that at one time, I took a lot of trout on bare hooks, 14s and 16s. The next stage was to build up a small thorax of silk (a little like the famous Sawyer Pheasant Tail pattern with a copper thorax). After all, the hook itself was thicker than the buzzer's body.

This experiment came to an end perforce one day at the Eye Brook. I'd had a marvellous day with my simple buzzers, and taken 16 fish when most other anglers had blanked. Back at the jetty, I made the mistake of showing my successful flies to some other anglers, It was quickly suggested that the bare shank made the 'flies' ideal as bait hooks. Things got very heated, and it was a relief when Robbo, the bailiff who lent his name to the cabin landmark at the 'Brook' intervened.

I explained what had taken place, and offered to let the two anglers inspect the boat, my bag, and tackle for hidden bait. Robbo, bless him, said this wasn't necessary, he knew me better than that, and sent the other two away with a flea in their ears. But when he saw the fly, with just a tiny olive ball of silk as a thorax, he suggested that a bare hook couldn't really be called a fly, and advised me that it would be best if I didn't use them in the future.

I adhered to his advice, but what I do insist on is a sparse, slim body on all my buzzer pupae. Without wishing to knock other fly suppliers, some of the commercial patterns are a disgrace. Yet these fatties still catch fish. The reason they do is interesting. It seems to me that a trout, mopping up buzzers in a shoal, is like a boy confronted with several cakes. His mates want the cakes too, and what he wants is the biggest one. So he grabs it. This explains why I've often had great success with a longshank 12 or 10 Seal's Fur Nymph of the right colour (and more recently the longshank BP), in the midst of a hatch of far smaller pupae. In fact the bigger the hatch, the more important it can be to give them something slightly different. The preoccupation of the buzzer-feeding trout is often with colour, and only sometimes with size.

At one time, at Grafham, and at the Eye Brook, we would see some really large buzzers. These now seem to be a thing of the past, perhaps fallen victim like a lot of aquatic insects to the effects of agricultural insecticides, blown or washed into the big reservoirs. Or are they? I well remember an evening when I fished at the Eye Brook, on what turned out to be a chilly July evening. A few sedges showed up, but the fish failed to respond in any great way, and by 7 pm I was shivering in my boat due to an unusually cold east wind. Going deepish with a sink tip I managed three fish, all of which were full of reddish brown buzzers. I stayed out to the last knockings, finishing off my session sitting over deep water, hoping for a rise from what I thought might be warmer water, less affected by the chilly breeze. Nothing happened. I was back early in the morning on the bank, and really struggled for one fish, as I waited to take out a boat. Around 8.30 am I got out on the water, and returning to my spot of the evening before, I found the surface thick with large buzzer shucks, up to an inch or more long. There certainly had been no hatch the evening before, nor that morning.

Obviously there had been a large hatch during the night. The fishing was very poor that morning, but I did manage two fish by going deep with a size 10 Cove Nymph. They contained one or two brown buzzers, but also a large amount of shucks. Clearly the fish had had a feast during the night, and somehow these two had missed out and were still hungry.

There *are* still some big buzzers about – but they hatch at night, and the trout enjoy a midnight beano, which no angler is allowed to see or fish to under present reservoir rules. Which is a pity, especially as big browns undoubtedly feed mainly in the hours of darkness.

Later on, we'll discuss where the nymph angler has to go next. With the certainty that these buzzers are hatching in very deep water, we'll talk about lead-lining with the nymph.

TACTICAL ROUND-UP

So many of our nymphing tactics have evolved specifically from buzzer fishing that the tactical section of this book could almost be subtitled 'fishing the buzzer'. But let's refresh our memories.

In the early-season cold, the fish, rather than the insects, lie deeper, and their main food when spooned very often turns out to be bloodworm, and dark buzzer pupae. Slow careful presentations of buzzer bloodworm combinations on a sink-tip – or on a dead drift with a floating line – will score. As the water warms, and fish and insect life livens up, fishing the top couple of feet of water becomes a more usual tactic.

We talked in the tactical chapter of various ways of fishing efficiently in the top water. But one thing I can't emphasise too strongly is the way that a matter of inches can make the difference on occasions. Take the experience of one of my fishing companions, *Trout Fisherman* magazine's Steve Windsor.

Fishing a match on Rutland Water in early June, he encountered a perfect nymphing day – a day when fish moved constantly, overcast, and with such a gentle breeze that despite the loch-style rules of the match, using a drogue, his boat partner, and Steve, were both able to fish nymphs. Steve fished an Intermediate in an attempt to make minimal line wake as there really wasn't much ripple. His partner started well, with a couple of fish, Steve caught one on a mini-lure, spooned it, and found that the main food was a mixture of olive nymphs, and olive coloured buzzers: on went an olive Fraser Nymph and Steve was very quickly four trout to two up. Then followed a dreadful two hour spell while his partner took six fish, and lost several others.

Having bagged up, his partner proved his sportsmanship by lending Steve his entire cast of flies – Soldier Palmer, well-chewed Pheasant Tail, and a Hare's Ear. Still Steve couldn't catch anything. The only problem either angler could think of was that blasted Intermediate. To save time, Steve rapidly greased the entire line, and immediately managed to hook two fish, and move several others. The difference can only have been a matter of inches; but it made all the difference.

All this is fine in a ripple, when you can grease the fly line tip, and quite a bit of the leader. But what do you do when the grease causes tell-tale ripples of wake on a calm surface?

This is the time when the Suspender Buzzer, or one of the Booby series nymphs comes into its own. A very slow figure-of-eight – and a degreased leader – will allow the other fly or flies to fish high in the water. That little foam bead or beads is just enough to keep the flies high. Stripping or pulling the Suspender Buzzer faster turns it into an effective wake lure – and not to my mind an imitation at all.

In a flat calm, quite a number of nymphs will get themselves glued in the surface film, half in and half out of their shucks, and struggling to get clear. Trout can cruise at will, sipping here and there. Many anglers will recommend using the Suspender Buzzer again, but to my mind, a buzzer hanging from the surface tail down, is not really an imitation of what the fish are picking up. When it actually hatches, the buzzer tips up and lies flat in the film, using the shuck as a little escape raft to stand on, drying its wings. If it gets stuck halfway it's still horizontal.

This is where the Damp Dries come in. Dressed in four basic buzzer colours, which are paler than the normal colours, with just an element therefore, of the air-filled shuck, and overlong waterlogged hackles, to suggest a straggle of trapped legs and wings, the flies have an extraordinary list of successes to their credit. The colours are grey duster, olive, ginger and black. Quite simply, when buzzer fishing, these are chucked out and left to fish, with perhaps the tiniest twitch every few minutes.

The flies I use, and their dressings – the Spiders, the Booby Nymphs, the Damp Dries, the BP's, the longshank Seal's Fur Nymphs, the Gold Ribbed Hare's Ears, the Bloodworms, the Buzzer Pupae, the Black Gnats, the Fraser Nymphs, the Cove Nymphs, and the Hackled Pheasant Tails – all have a role to play in buzzer fishing. If nothing else, they emphasise the vast importance of the buzzer to the modern reservoir nymph angler.

5 · THE SEDGE – NOT JUST A FLY FOR SUMMER

A lake in winter may seem as dead and still as the grave. Ice clings in the margins, and only sturdy rushes are left of the luscious growth of summer weed. It's hard to believe that any trace is left of the skimming, clumsily flying sedge hordes of those long summer nights, but below the water surface, clinging to the weeds and submerged undergrowth, or crawling slowly and awkwardly along the bottom, the cased caddis of the sedge remains. Safe in his sleeping bag of grit or twig, he sifts the silt for his breakfast.

Come the spring he'll be a little more active, and while he'll sit unmoving in one position for long periods like some ancient Pharaoh in a mummy case, now and again he will stir. Hungry trout, keen to pack on weight for a minimum of effort, adore the sluggish sedge larva and crunch him down, case and all. Nor is it unusual to find that the trout has made a mistake, and boasts a bellyful of twigs.

This says a lot for the camouflage of the caddis: twigs, small stones, bits of sand like grit, hollow sections of flood-killed grass or bankside rushes, in fact almost anything the caddis has handy, are all woven together with its superglue secretions, and form home, shield and disguise to what, unclothed, is a plump and tempting little maggot-like creature. Oddly enough 'nude' caddis are often a bright almost fluorescent green. There are a huge variety of sedges, in many sizes, from a mere fraction of an inch, up to an inch or more. That said, few English anglers will encounter

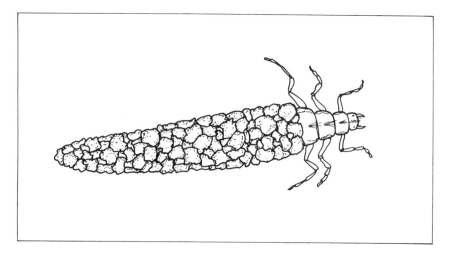

Fig 15

Cased caddis or sedge larva (Limnephilus flavicornis)

anything the size of the Irish Murragh, a good inch or more in length. There are also some free-swimming caddis larvae, but I have yet to recognise one in the fish I've spooned.

The larva of the insect known as *Trichoptera* in Latin, and as sedge or caddis fly to the angler, is an important source of food in the early season, and all year through, (like the *corixa* and bloodworm, odd ones always seem to turn up in spoonings), but the great hatches that sometimes delight the summer nymph angler are less common. From late May through to September you may encounter a hatch. When you do, the trout will often feed hungrily on what seems to be a plumply tempting little pupa. But like the large buzzers, good sedge hatches seem to be less and less common these days. One thing is certain – a great many sedges hatch in the hours of darkness, and many a classic evening rise that has held bank anglers long after the light has gone, and the boats were in, has been caused by the sedge coming off in large numbers. (Outside the context of this book, the adult makes such a spectacle of itself, waking across the top while trying to get off the water, that a dry fly can be deadly on occasions.) A nice plump sedge with its big wings struggling to get out of its pupal case, must make a superb target for a hungry trout.

TACTICS FOR THE CASED CADDIS

As I've said, if there's little other food around early in the season, trout will often feed on caddis for several weeks. Now, no caddis ever whizzed about at any great speed. Despite that obvious fact, a caddis moved quickly, especially a non-specific pattern like the Baddow, makes an excellent lure.

But to be cleverer than that, we want to be a little imitative. We want to get our caddis down deep, and keep it there. I use only two patterns (you could go crazy copying every caddis you saw), my Eye Brook Caddis, size 10 to 14 and a longshank Hare's Ear, dressed on longshank from size 10 to 12. Both are generally leaded, and, using a floater or sink-tip, the retrieve needs to be just fast enough to keep the nymph from bouncing bottom too often.

Try to remember the areas where sedge hatches were prolific last year, because it's here we should find the heaviest numbers of cased caddis in the spring. At the 'Brook' there's an area known as Pollard's Jump. One year in late April, I encountered a lovely spring day, sunshine, and no wind, and I was able to fish in shirt sleeves. Of course the weather was hardly ideal for fishing. After an hour of grubbing along fruitlessly with various buzzer patterns near the bottom, I took a break. I tied on an Eye Brook Caddis. Chucking it out into the flat calm I settled down for my 20 minute break.

When I picked up the rod again, and began to retrieve my floater, I soon encountered resistance. Lifting, I found myself fast into a brown of 1¼ lb. After a firm tap on its head, I went to unhook it. To my amazement all I saw was the line disappearing down its throat. I had to gut the fish to get my fly back, and it was full of what looked like half-inch-long twigs. They were neat caddis cases made of sand, their colour almost identical to my nymph.

I started fishing again and despite a degreased leader, I had to leave the caddis a couple of minutes to sink, then use the slowest figure-of-eight retrieve to fish the fly. That meant a single turn of the hand every 15 or 20 seconds. A take was just like hooking bottom: the line would go heavy, and I'd tighten up. Sometimes it was bottom, sometimes a fish. I was delighted with a catch of nine browns that day. All, when gutted, were stuffed with cased caddis. There's no doubt that where you do find them, cased caddis can appear in huge numbers.

65

TACTICS FOR THE PUPA

On the day that the sedge larva pupates, it moves a stage further up the trout's menu. Free swimming, it moves well in the water, which is no surprise. After a year or more in its case as larva, the pupa carves its way out, and heads one way – for the surface and hatching. Its skin swells with gas as it goes, which may accelerate its upward movement, and certainly assists the adult in its escape from the shuck. It can hatch very fast if all goes well – and, as I've said, the adult then whizzes equally rapidly across the surface to flight. It has also been suggested that some species crawl up weed stems to hatch. Either way, the trout can intercept the pupa at any stage of its upward journey.

This fast-hatching process allows the angler to use a faster retrieve than many other nymphing styles. If the trout are taking deep, a speed of a couple of yards of line a minute; if they're higher up, a faster figure-of-eight, or a series of steady 2 foot draws seems effective. When a really good hatch is taking place, I'm not averse to my dropper fly waking on the surface slightly, for the reasons I've just outlined.

A simple brown or yellow seal's fur Palmer can be deadly on the dropper. On the point by far the most productive colour for the Hatching Sedge is pale yellow, though greens, ambers, cream, and gingers are all

Fig 16

Sedge pupa

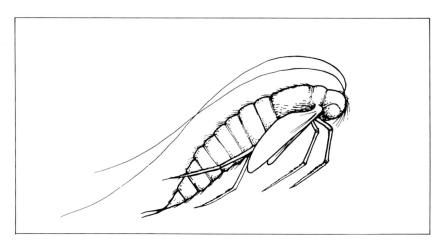

worth a try. Exaggerating the size can work too, which is one place where the longshank Invicta Nymph comes in.

Not many seasons back, I fished at Rutland with my son Shaun. The Green Bank area was fishing well, in the sense that the fish were plentiful, but not easy to catch. The fish would move in about 8 pm, and on the night in question, around 20 anglers in the area only took a dozen or so fish. Shaun got a nice brown of around 3 lb on a buzzer but all I could manage was a couple of fish lost on Fraser Nymphs.

Later that night we gutted Shaun's fish, to find it full of pale yellow sedge pupae. I spent a couple of hours next morning, matching different materials to the pupae, and finally when rayon floss and mixed seal's fur did the trick, I tied up four flies. I carried on with the day's orders, but found that the itch became too strong. Around 4 pm I made up my mind, and decided to see if the new pattern would work. It took two seconds to persuade Shaun to join me, and half an hour later we were tackling up on the Green Bank.

Not much happened again until 8 pm when the wind dropped, and the fish moved in. Eventually there were fish showing everywhere. Through the fading light Shaun had tried various patterns without success, and I'd picked up an early fish on an Invicta Nymph. The time was right, and I tied on one of the new patterns, after taking two down to Shaun. He was getting knocks on the Invicta Nymph and stuck with it for a while. With a new pattern on the point, and a Palmer on the dropper, I went back to my spot. I started my figure-of-eight with the flies right on the top, and around the fourth cast a fish came to inspect the flies. He popped up behind the Palmer, appeared to turn away in disgust, then everything went solid and I had a fighting rainbow of about 2 lb on the end. It had the Hatching Sedge firmly in its mouth, and a bellyful of the yellow sedge pupae when spooned.

Shortly afterwards I got a second rainbow of the same size. Shaun asked if it took the new fly, and promptly tied one on. The fish killed, I turned back to the water, only to hear a crack, and a curse from Shaun (don't look at me, I didn't teach him that!). He'd had an instant take and cracked the fly off striking too hard. Something told me that there were good fish around, and short of flies as we were, I advised him to tighten more gently. In a short time, Shaun had four fish, and I had six. A couple approached to find out what the 'new' pattern was. They even wanted to

One of Gordon's customers, Rod Woolnough lets his face say it all as he weighs in a five pound rainbow taken on one of Gordon's imitative flies in a heavy dusk rise.

buy one. In fact, one of the anglers offered me £1 a fly. With just one spare, I refused.

Just after this I hooked a really good fish, even for Rutland. It was a huge rainbow that would have broken the fishery record I suspect. After about ten minutes of fun and games, I got it into the margins. At this stage I got a bit careless. Never try to net a big fish before it's ready. I did, and with one flick of its chunky tail it was gone. It had snapped the leader, and taken another precious fly.

There's nothing to match the sickening feeling of seeing a big fish of a lifetime swim away, because of your own stupidity. We continued fishing, and managed a limit apiece by 9.30 pm. What a baptism for a new pattern. As we were packing up the two unhappy anglers came back, one having taken a fish on an Invicta, the other fishless. We gave them the remaining patterns, and they cheered up a bit. For the others on the Green Bank it had been just the odd fish. But one of the anglers we gave the flies to called me the next evening, with thanks. He ordered some more nymphs – the two originals had taken them three fish apiece, including a superb 6½ lb brown. Another triumph for the nymph, and imitative fishing!

6 · THE OLIVE – A SPRING AND AUTUMN FAVOURITE

The English stillwater angler will mostly encounter the pond olive and the lake olive. Over the whole of the UK, he may also come across the sepia dun, and the claret dun. All are part of the much larger Ephemeroptera family that includes the mayfly at the large end, and the *caenis* at the tiny. Indeed, to the Americans the whole family is known as the mayflies. Just to confuse the issue, the British angler may occasionally refer to the dayflies, a reference to the short adult lives of this fly. All this matters little to the stillwater angler, who'll find the adult olives unmistakeable, and the nymphs almost identical.

A hatch of olives is impossible to miss, as the adult fly sits with its sail-like wings erect, and is blown along by the wind for some time, before taking off. The colder the weather, the longer the adult may sit.

Unlike the buzzer and the sedge, the olive has no larval stage, so the nymph angler is mainly concerned with just one sub-aquatic form – although, like the buzzer, the olives often get stuck at the surface, and a hatching pattern can be very useful, as we'll see.

HABITAT AND BEHAVIOUR

The pond and lake olive nymphs are free-swimming and can move at quite a speed. Generally of a brown colour somewhere between beige and chestnut, they also sometimes have touches of green about the body.

70

Fig 17

Pond olive nymph (Cloeon dipterum)

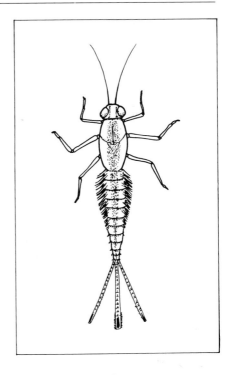

Though I certainly wouldn't be able to tell them apart, the pond olive prefers the shallows, the lake olive the deeper water.

On most British waters you can expect the pond and lake olives to appear from mid-April in a warm year, and peak in May, and again, in September. The pond olive is smaller in September, while the lake olive seems to appear in only one size through the season. I say through, because there always appears to be a smattering of olives around, once they first show. Often they'll hatch alongside the buzzers, and fish seem to like a mixed diet of both, picking them off in almost equal proportions – though in numbers, the olives never quite seem to match the buzzers.

It's quite usual to see the adults sailing along over quite deep water, but as a rule, the best sport will come in water up to 10 feet deep. Many writers have placed the olives right at the top of the trout's feeding list: I can't help feeling that that idea has washed over from running water, where they undoubtedly top the list. In most stillwaters, however, they come after buzzers, sedges and daphnia, with slight variations from water to water. Seasonally, olives may also become first choice.

71

Early September on the Eye Brook, and an olive Fraser Nymph brings Gordon's first fish of the day from the weeds.

FLIES AND TACTICS

For what it's worth, I can easily describe the progress of the olive at Eye Brook. The early hatches are rather large and dark, through the mid-season they pale off, and by September a smaller almost ginger hatch appears.

We must match our patterns accordingly. Pheasant tail seems to be a universal material for olive nymphs, and there's no doubt that both the

72

Cove Nymph, or a Sawyer-style pheasant tail (tied like the Fraser Nymph, with legs and tails), will take their share of olive-feeding fish. But since the discovery of the Fraser Nymph, which was originally tied to copy some large buff-coloured buzzers, in a similar style to the Sawyer pheasant tails, I've rarely used anything else in a hatch of olives. As we'll see later, it's still pheasant tail, but the paler hen pheasant, that's so deadly. And the addition of a green rib and thorax adds an alternative tinge of olive, which on some days also scores well.

Not especially original, but new to me, and very deadly, is my Hackled Pheasant Tail, either in standard cock pheasant, or in a bleached ginger shade. This later fly had an incredible impact when first tested, and has proved itself essential from August onwards. The standard unbleached pattern can be hackled with brown, olive, or blue dun, to suit the hatch.

Very useful indeed are mole Spiders in olive, yellow, ginger, and brown, and the Gold Ribbed Hare's Ear in small sizes, and in my mixed blended fur version.

Another nymph new to my list, and rapidly ousting even the Fraser Nymph is a longshank 12 BP nymph. Fawn, fiery brown, olive, ginger and yellow are all worth trying. Like the buzzer, on some days exact sizes don't seem important, and can even cut down your success rate. I've known days when 10 longshanks beat more accurately sized 14s and 16s, but as a rule, size 12 and 14 longshank flies are what I'll end up using in an olive hatch. Late in the season the little ginger fly calls for 14s and 16s, on standard hooks.

As the buzzer often is, but to an even greater extent, the olive seems to be a nine to five fly. When there's no sign of a rise at the times I know olives are on the menu, I start with a pair of Fraser Nymphs on the usual long leader, well rubbed down with mud. I'll try a 12 longshank on the point, and a 14 on the dropper, perhaps mixing the Olive and the standard Fraser Nymphs. You can also use a similar retrieve to the *corixa* tactics we'll look at later, but with the sink-and-draw slightly less exaggerated. A 2 foot, fairly swift figure-of-eight, followed by a few second's pause, gives a lifelike movement. You can fish a little faster with the Olive than many other nymphs: as I mentioned before, they're fast and efficient swimmers.

Perhaps for this reason trout tend to show when they're feeding high on the water on olive nymphs, by taking the fly at the surface with a hurried splashy rise. When this happens, I start the retrieve as soon as the flies hit the surface, and may even start the retrieve with smooth steady draws of 2 feet or more, and virtually no pause at all. It's also the time to sort out a few Hackled Pheasant Tails and pop one on the dropper.

If you still don't start to catch (and you're sure that olives are causing the rise – which you will be, when those little galleons start to blow down the wind) it's probably time to carefully grease-up the leader. Don't overdo this. Although when grease is needed, you can't get by without it. I vividly recall a day on the Eye Brook in mid-May. I started a few days' holiday on the Monday, and took out a boat. There was a gentle warm southerly wind, and it was overcast. In fact, apart from a steady drizzle, fishing conditions were near perfect.

I headed for a favourite area by the Bird Hide, happily noting the swifts and martins feasting on the hatching flies. As so often happens when nature lays a table for a feast, everyone was joining in, and I must have seen a dozen trout move in the first 10 minutes, many in casting range.

Full of confidence, I tackled up with a floater, usual long leader well rubbed down with mud, and a pair of Fraser Nymphs. I was about 100 yards offshore, in 10 feet of water, with a lovely nymphing wave rolling past the anchored boat, and after a breather and a cup of coffee, I began to fish round in front of me, first up in the top few inches, then a little deeper. After about 10 minutes, a steady draw brought me a brown of about a pound, which when spooned contained dark olive nymphs and a few buzzers. By 4 pm I was well content with eight nice fish, all on Fraser Nymphs, and I left early to take out my wife Margaret.

Two days later, in identical and unchanged conditions, I was back at the water chafing at the bit for some more excellent nymphing. I dropped anchor in the same spot. The birds were there stuffing themselves, and the trout were moving. This, I told myself, would be easy.

Fishing in the same manner as I had on the Monday, I went through a variety of retrieves, and even tried other nymphs, expecting the same results. After a blank hour, I was really worried; by one in the afternoon, I'd even tried a Black Lure without success. All confidence gone, I reeled in and ate some lunch. All morning there had been olives drifting by, and fish showing. So what was wrong?

I tied on a fresh dry Fraser Nymph, and cast out. The flies hit the water, there was a swirl, and I was into a fish. Marvellous! Ever-so-gently

I played out the fish, finally netting it safely. The spoon showed it to be full of olive nymphs, just like all of Monday's fish. What had I been doing wrong? My mind turned to the lure I had just taken off, and the *dry* nymph I'd tied to my *dry* leader. It had to be the difference.

I lightly greased the leader, but immediately saw that a standard retrieve made the leader wake and stick out like a sore thumb. So I cast across the wind, and fished more slowly than usual with a gentle figure-of-eight. About three casts later there was a swirl by the leader, the line drew away, and I was into another fish. By 6 pm I had nine fish.

Without grease I'm certain I wouldn't have touched more fish that day. Why had the feeding habit changed? I can only conclude that over three days of steady feeding the fish were into the habit of taking the easily-caught hatching nymphs at the surface, not the faster, free-swimming nymphs below. So high in the water were their noses that I'd been fishing below them.

This pattern of feeding also occurs, as we've seen, with buzzers, and can occur with sedges, and even snails! Don't fall into the same trap that I did.

Perhaps the most difficult trout to catch is one feeding on a sparse hatch of olives, moving quietly up the wind, and just showing here and there. As I've said, it's not at all unusual for there to be a sparse hatch of olives trickling off through the day. Trout will suddenly appear moving slowly up the wind, and rising here and there. Sometimes their diet is entirely of olive nymphs and trapped emerging adults, and on other occasions they'll contain a mixture of flies, and other bugs, but with a majority of olives.

This feeding pattern may occur on almost any day of the season, and even while other fish are feeding exclusively on, say, *corixa*, or dead fry, there's always likely to be a fish over the more open water, showing just once here and there.

On one spectacular occasion my boat partner had barely tied on a Muddler to a floating line when the only fish that had showed all day popped up in easy casting range just yards from the boat, and over deep water. It took the stripped muddler with a firm swirl first time, and when spooned contained a couple of *corixa*, and several olive nymphs. You could almost map the path of that fish, from the weedbeds on the far bank up to the deeper water near the Eye Brook dam at Harrison's Corner.

These 'oncers' as they are often called have some funny feeding habits as two stories will illustrate. Both happened to Steve Windsor in the 1985 season.

The first incident was at Rutland in June. Fish were showing in a regular but disordered way. A fish would rise well clear of the boat, then pop up again almost underneath it. The only apparent governing factor of their movements was that they were coming diagonally across, and not straight into the gentle wind. Their movement was right to left across the front of the drifting boat, and it was very hard to develop the habit of peering wide to your right for a rising fish that might eventually pop up in front of the boat in a castable-to position. So it was often a case of casting blind, and without much success. Still a bag of fish was gradually being built up.

In calms like this Steve often fishes a 4 weight line and light rod. Pitching the line out to his right, so that it would come round well clear of the boat, Steve paused to grab a mouthful of food. With his hand in the bag, he could have sworn that he noticed the line suddenly slide away from him. He put it down to the motion of the boat, and grabbed a few more mouthfuls. Picking up the rod, everything was solid. Obviously a trout had taken the fly, a very ragged well-chewed and tailless Fraser Nymph on the dead sink. It was hooked well down the throat. Interestingly, the drag of the light line had not put the fish off, but had been enough to hold the point of the hook sufficiently pricked into the fish to ensure that it couldn't spit the fly.

As if this wasn't enough, Steve's boat partner had exactly the same thing happen an hour or so later. And as, on this occasion, his line was cast out in front of the boat dead straight, the fly must have been virtually motionless. It should then have been easy to cast to an approaching fish, let all sink slowly, and wait for the line movement. Unfortunately those darned 'oncers' would not come down the wind like normal fish, nor show regularly enough as they moved in from the right hand side to allow an accurate cast. All the fish had a mixed spooning, with a majority of olive nymphs.

September saw Steve and I struggling on one of the rare sunny days in 1985. The Eye Brook, which had fished well a few days before was in one of its difficult moods. We'd fished all over for four trout, taken on both a floater, and a deep-sunk lure. Steve had even broken a favourite rod in mid-cast. Thoroughly annoyed, he'd set up a toothpick of a river rod,

76

with a 3 lb leader and a tiny dry fly, to cast at some enormous roach that were rolling around on the surface. He'd not succeeded, but with a size 16 Pheasant Tail dry on the light leader, we moved the boat down to the Bell. Here some trout were enjoying a casual evening rise, dimpling here and there.

Seeing the rises, Steve picked up the light rod, and flicked a short cast to a fish that showed. Up it came like a gentleman and rolled over the dry fly. On 3 lb line and with nearby weeds, three minutes of lunacy followed before a fit-looking cock rainbow joined us in the boat. With our usual attitude to 'dry fly' fishing, Steve didn't bother to dry the fly, simply false cast a few times, and pitched the fly out again. After a few minutes it just dipped under the surface. Immediately there was a swirl, and Steve's bright yellow leader butt cut through the water. A lift, and . . . nothing. Just like the pulls to a sinking bloodworm, the takes weren't easy to hit.

In disgust Steve lifted off and flicked the fly back into the water. The dry fly sank slowly, and after a few seconds, away went the leader – this time with no indication of a rise at all. A lift, and a long slow fight saw a 2 lb-plus rainbow eventually in the boat.

These takes to the slowly sinking nymph (or a swamped dry fly which has become a 'nymph') are harder to account for than the takes to sinking bloodworms falling from the weed. Could it be that the adult insect that doesn't make a clean hatch actually begins to slowly sink down in the water? Or does the hatching olive actually start the process below the surface? Certainly we only observe this behaviour with olive-feeding trout.

Another point worth mentioning here is that the fish that take on the drop often seem, like Steve's two Eye Brook trout, to be fish that have been in the water for some time. Have they perhaps got wise to the pulled retrieves preferring to trust a static fly more than a moving one? If so, it's not surprising that my dead drift tactics with nymphs have always outscored those with retrieved flies, and that the takes are more confident with this method. Certainly I'd chance pitching a nymph to a rising trout and doing simply nothing but watching the line for a steady draw. Especially with the olives, it seems that there are occasions when no presentation is the best presentation of all.

7 · THE CORIXA – THE BANK ANGLER'S BEST FRIEND

The *corixa* is defined by the aquatic entomologists as a bug. That's a useful reference point for the stillwater flyfisherman too.

I first came across this interesting little creature when I did a rare thing for me and fished the Eye Brook on opening day. The only spot I could get was the ditch about 300 yards up from the bottom of Stoke Dry road towards the entry of the creek. I struggled a bit, but took a fish on a Black Lure. Spooning it later I found it was stuffed to the gills with *corixa*. Tying up what I thought was a fair imitation, I went back the next day and managed seven trout. But it's not just at the start of the season that the bug is a useful nymph. This is one nymph that's a standby for the whole season through. Even then it seems to peak in early May and towards the end, when the buzzers are around in fewer numbers.

There are some 36 varieties of *corixa*, and as it's an air breather, rising to the surface and returning with a silvery aqualung skin of air around its body, it doesn't need superb conditions to survive. It also flies and will colonise any new semi-permanent puddle given the chance. As a consequence it's found in virtually every trout fishery in the country.

Don't confuse the *corixa* with the much larger and upside down water boatman that swims on its back and hunts at the surface. The *corixa* eats any rotting matter on the bottom, and probably serves as a useful scavenger. A group of them will even gnaw away at a dead fish. Its beetle form is quite easily identifiable, with its slightly marbled dark brown back, distinctive round head, and sharply angled legs. Though there are larger

Note the true size of the corixa spooned from a fish taken in the Weedy Blood's Dyke area of the Eye Brook. Gordon's imitation is a perfect match.

specimens, the trout definitely prefer the 12-14 hook-sized natural.

While not top of the trouty menu on some waters, there seems to be virtually no time when the trout won't take them, and they turn up in spoonings all year through. Don't worry about identifying between the various species as the differences are minute, and the only change from place to place may be in the belly colour, which can be pale green or dirty white, but most often seems to be dirty yellow. Those sticking-out legs remain impossible to miss, as it swims the breaststroke.

HABITAT

Corixa prefer sheltered and shallow water, most often in the vicinity of weed beds, or in the early season, over the remains of last year's rotten weed beds. It's usually a waste of time to fish this pattern over very deep or open water, except during a summer kill. Trout feeding on *corixa* are often seen coming out like missiles after the bug, as they chase it to the surface in shallow water. Weedbeds, ditches, and sunken hedges provide the *corixa* with cover.

TACKLE

A standard fly rod and a floating line should suffice on most occasions. The leader will need to be between 12 and 15 feet long to fish the fly efficiently. Match the breaking strain of the nylon to the area you plan to fish. At Eye Brook and other weedy waters you'll be hauling fish through weed. Even then I rarely go over 6 lb. From a boat you may get away with lighter nylon.

TACTICS

METHOD ONE – IN THE WEEDS

It's the *corixa*'s need to rise up for surface air that makes it both susceptible to the trout, and easy to imitate for the nymph fisherman. At one time I fished entirely with a dirty-yellow-bodied *corixa* – which is certainly the most common colour on the Midland lakes. Now I also favour a silver version, to imitate the 'shuck' of air the bug pulls down with it. The earlier floss versions took bubbles of air *down* with them, I think.

I fish just one fly – nice straightforward fishing this, and as we're in the weedbeds, droppers are risky anyway – and grease up the last 2 feet of my fly line. The leader on the other hand is degreased for a fast sink, with the clay I mentioned earlier. This, I hope, enables me to get a vertical lift.

I fish the fly sink-and-draw. This silver version logically should get more takes on the drop, so cast out, tighten up, and watch for a pull while the bug sinks. These slow draws are usually hard to miss.

It might take a minute for this comparatively small pattern to get down 6 feet, so be patient. I then retrieve with a fast figure-of-eight, bringing in about 8 feet of line, then repeat the process. Takes are usually very positive and all that's necessary is to set the hook. Don't strike hard, a simple lift (as in most cases) will set the hook. As I've often said, ex-coarse fishermen who strike at floats are the worst offenders at this. If you strike hard into a moving fish, don't blame your nylon for a break! Continue the sink-and-draw, covering as wide an area as possible, and fishing each cast right out into the margins. At Eye Brook where you may be wading thigh deep in weed with a covering band of weed in front of you, you may take fish right under the rod tip.

METHOD TWO – VERY SHALLOW WATER

In shallow water, you should not need to grease the fly line. In fact in 4 or 5 feet of water you can get the ultimate smooth retrieve by fishing a true sink-and-draw, and lifting the rod to retrieve, tightening up as the fly sinks then repeating the lift.

On hard fished small clearwater fisheries where the fish will be sick of the sight of giant leaded nymphs (some of which will purport to be *corixa* too), you can put the small delicate copy near them and they'll often have it. Best of all, pitch it between two cruising fish, and do that subtle rod lift. The chances are that one of the competing fish will have it.

METHOD THREE – THE DEEP CORIXA

Corixa also grub about on the bottom, and, early in the season when there's little weed, I like to grub a couple of artificials along the bottom. An 18 foot leader with two flies on it, one 8 feet up from the point, will do the job. On the point a leaded yellow or beige *corixa*, an unleaded version on the dropper, or one of the seasonal nymphs, like a sedge pupa or buzzer.

Again, look for takes on the drop. Then slowly retrieve in foot-long pulls, with a few seconds' pause between pulls. Takes, again, are usually unmistakeable. As on most occasions, I don't look for takes but feel for them.

METHOD FOUR – THE DEEP DRIFT

A second option with this rig is to cast across the wind, and let it swing the line and flies around. This is a lazy method but can produce the perfect slow presentation. Follow the line around with the rod tip, and tighten by moving the rod smoothly to one side – don't try to lift off all that line in a bow, at once.

In a fairly fresh wind, you'll need a well-leaded point fly to maintain the depth, and in a faster drift, a sink tip comes in handy, keeping the flies really deep.

METHOD FIVE – THE MIDSUMMER SURFACE CORIXA

A strange phenomenon often occurs with *corixa* in midsummer, when they suddenly seem to die off *en masse*, and being buoyant, rise to the surface before floating away across the water in large numbers. In 1976 at the Eye Brook you could see thousands of corpses washed up, many of apparently immature *corixa*. Perhaps a population explosion plays a part? The trout and waterside birds had a field day: so did some lucky anglers.

If this phenomenon occurs where you fish, get out the faithful floater, and with an 18 foot leader and pair of unleaded flies (slightly smaller than usual – 14s perhaps), grease up the whole leader except the dropper. If you fish from the bank, choose a spot with a back wind and let the flies drift slowly out offshore, after casting along the bank. You can if you wish let out extra line, and drift the flies a long way out. Then, commence a fast figure-of-eight retrieve, and as often happens with drifting or surface flies, look out for sharp fast takes. It can even pay to hold your rod up slightly, normally a fault, as despite the fast retrieve this will still give the trout a chance to turn down with the fly. Even though your retrieved *corixa* will be going against the drift, the trout will often have it.

NOW LET'S GO FISHING

It's early August, and knowing what the trout are about at this time of the year, we needn't plan too early a start. About 8 am on the bank should suffice if the weather is kind and not too bright.

There's not too much of a breeze, but what there is has been blowing down the reservoir from the weedy end all week. They stocked a couple of days ago, and by now a lot of the fish that are left after the lure rippers have had their share are running down the wind towards the weedy end.

In typical corixa water, Gordon has boldly gone where no angler has been before. The apparently unfishable spots yield the better quality fish, to anglers prepared to play fish carefully while stood a rod's length from the water's edge.

If we want to avoid them we'll have to be careful and fish our nymphs intelligently. The water's still fairly warm and fish are moving at all depths, but the shallows have been warm the longest, and this area has long been well-worth nymphing. Still, there's not a lot of activity among the weed beds at first sight, and certainly no buzzer hatch.

We'll tackle up the usual rods with floating lines. No need to go too heavy among these beds of ranunculus – most fish will fight clear of them, especially rainbows, and we wouldn't be able to pull them through on 10 lb, if we were daft enough to try. Instead we'll let them fight out in the open, then lift them gently over the weed. We'll probably lose one or two, but mostly as they fall off – never with hooks in them.

This is one place where I'll wade more or less straight in. A likely spot

83

will be where I can wade out through the weed, cast into open water, and still have a few safe inches of wader clear of the water. Watch out for soft mud, though.

Once in position, with a long-handled net lying on the thick weeds close to hand, I'll put a leaded Corixa on the point and will chance a dropper with a buzzer pattern on it this time. That sink-and-draw will bring the buzzer up in hatching fashion, while the Corixa acts just as naturally. With a last rub down of the line tip with grease, I check the knots, and carefully work out line clear of the weeds before casting.

Giving a good long pull with the left hand to tighten everything up, I glance around at the water beneath my feet. As the cloud of my mud clears, I can see quite a few fry hiding in the weed roots. Later in the season a floating fry with a *corixa* (or other nymph) suspended below it will cover both options. It might even work today, too.

But there too, whizzing up to the surface, is a *corixa*, and below it syphoning the mud are several others. Blast, missed! I was so busy looking below, that my mind wandered from the fly. So the trout are here, and so totally preoccupied with *corixa* that they will take the fly on the drop. Another cast or three and a fish takes solidly as the fly rises. Then another, and another and I take off the buzzer, and put a yellow Corixa on the point, leaded, and a silver on the dropper. More fish follow.

About 5 pm, a couple of friends arrive from work, and seeing the fish, and the results of my spoonings – choc-a-bloc with *corixa* – they tackle up and wade in. Lots of space up here, as most bank anglers fear the weed too much to fish it. About now the wind starts to drop and a fish or two begins to rise and hopes go higher. But then first one, then another speck of white dust appears on our sleeves. It's the dreaded angler's curse . . . *caenis*.

I wade out of the water, and watch as gradually the whole surface of the lake becomes dimpled with rising fish. Fish that, as my two friends find, are impossible to catch. I don't wait and watch them struggle. With a handy seven fish, it's more than time to get home and do some work on the tying bench. After all, for those in the know, the Corixa is much in demand at this time of the year.

8 · LARGE NYMPHS

Most of the creatures we imitate when we fish the nymph have some large insects in their families, and some small. Buzzers and sedges range from a fraction of an inch to an inch or more long, but when it comes to the really meaty items in the trout's diet, we have to look to the underwater bandits: damselfly and dragonfly nymphs, and the alder nymph, all of which eat a fair few nymphs, and other smaller creatures, themselves.

The alder larva, unlike the other two, changes its habits when it transforms itself into an adult. Its sedge-like form is often seen in May, basking calmly in the sun. It's much darker than a sedge, but often mistaken for one. The adult is not a trouty delicacy (though some will say it's eaten regularly, being a weak flier), but the nymph apparently forms a major part of the early-season diet of some trout.

I say apparently because despite its legendary appearance, I've rarely spooned one from a fish. Although there are special patterns, a leaded longshank Hare's Ear, fished slow and deep, should suffice if your spoon brings one of these dark brown vicious-jawed predators from a trout's stomach.

Dragonfly larvae are even bigger and chunkier. But I've yet to find one of these making a hearty meal for a trout. Which brings us to the damselfly, the slim, vicious, pirate of the air, and its equally hungry larvae.

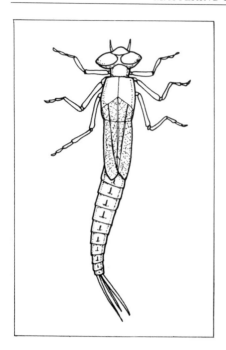

Fig 18

Damsel-fly nymph (Agrion virgo)

THE DAMSEL NYMPH

We've all seen the beautiful and very common blue damselflies humming over any clean piece of water. They can snatch another insect in flight, with an aggression that belies their beauty. Their carefully laid eggs hatch into what eventually becomes a nymph of an inch or more in length, ranging in colour from pale brown through to dark olive green – the olive variety being by far the most common.

HABITAT

Like a lot of predators, the damsel nymph hangs about in dark corners of the weedbeds, waiting to sneak out and grab his breakfast with a particularly vicious pair of pincers. For this he can produce a pretty good turn of speed by waggling his body and the fan-shaped breathers on his tail. In June or July, he climbs up a weed stalk, splits his coat and emerges eventually as an accomplished flier – rather like a submarine suddenly becoming a fighter plane.

The hatches often happen in large numbers, and the trout can take advantage. Look for a fish nudging a weedbed, and among the likely targets are damsel nymphs. It's not easy to imitate a nymph crawling up a rush, but when a damsel's flushed and takes to free-swimming – then we have a chance.

TACKLE

Very standard – by June the nymphs start to move inshore, and that means shallow water and floating lines. A little lead in one of my brown and green longshank Seal's Fur Nymphs will get the buoyant seal's fur down quickly, and keep it there. Good dropper patterns in early June would include almost anything except perhaps sedges. I'd ring the changes with a variety of Spiders.

TACTICS

Pitching in the holes among the weedbeds can produce results at this time of the year, as we've seen in the tactical section. The Brown and Green longshank may well score. Damsels seem to have a distinct preference for the cleaner spring-fed water of gravel pits, yet they can be found on the large reservoirs too.

The secret is to fish among the weedbeds they inhabit. As we can't imitate their crawl among the weeds, we must try to copy their panic as they're flushed. A fast smooth figure-of-eight will fish the fly in a very natural way, which is why the lead comes in handy – giving the fly some depth when it's fished at speed.

I fish a lot with Steve Windsor of *Trout Fisherman* magazine. Steve remembers a day at Ringstead when the damsel came up trumps for him. It was a competition day, and the morning sport had been excellent: Steve had been especially lucky and lay second. The afternoon was a different kettle of trout. Sport had slowed, and, needing only ounces to stay in touch, Steve wandered the bank looking for a couple of fish to catch up. In the far corner from the lodge by the road, there was a weedbed a long way out. With a back wind, and 40 yards to cast, Steve finally managed to drop the Damselfly Nymph so that it just touched the weed. He then put the rod under his arm and started a swift hand-over-hand retrieve. After

With a good fish on, Shaun Fraser applies extra pressure with the left hand.

about six hand movements the line tightened, and swinging his body round he hooked a super rainbow of 2½ lb. What impressed him was that the area had been heavily fished with nymph and lure all day. But getting the correct presentation and the right fly had fooled a nice fish.

It would be nice to report he won the match – but it wasn't enough.

It's hard to spot damsel-feeding fish. But bear in mind that from June to September the natural is around, and that the artificial will nearly always stand a chance when fish are just moving around taking whatever comes handy. Interestingly enough, I've heard that the bright blue 'nymphs' that in some way resemble the adults, are also seeing a lot of

Here's the fish Shaun Fraser needed two hands to land. His last fish of the 1986 season, it was a fin-perfect rainbow.

success on small southern waters – notably Damerham in Hampshire – fished wet of course!

THE MAYFLY

We've talked a lot about the smaller brothers of this giant ephemerid, the various olives. It's hard to believe that this large creamy nymph could ever be a relative, and when it's remembered that it's related to the microscopic *caenis* too, it seems even harder to believe. Ten years ago, this book would never have mentioned the mayfly, but the recent conversion of the small, often chalkstream-fed, southern waters into trout fisheries, with regular hatches, changed all that. Draw a line from Bristol to the Wash, and every hole in the ground suddenly seems to claim a hatch.

The truth is that the muddy walls of many of the small fisheries provide ideal little caverns for the nymph to bore into. Formerly threatened populations have suddenly found a refuge, and have grown. Some large reservoirs feature a mayfly hatch too. There's a spectacular one at Tittesworth in North Staffordshire.

The main species most anglers think of when they hear the word mayfly is *Ephemera danica*, a creamy yellow and dark brown in both nymph and adult. But the hatch at Tittesworth is of *Ephemera vulgata*, a species in which dark brown and yellow bands combine differently to produce what at first sight is an olive green fly.

TACKLE

As for the Damselfly: grubbing one of these slow and deep seems to produce results even on waters where the mayfly is never seen, so a long leader with a floating line, and a leaded pattern on the point usually does the trick. Like the damselfly Green and Brown Nymph, my Mayfly Nymph is an excellent pattern for picking off cruising fish in small clear water fisheries. Fish them as described in the tactical chapter. (Chapter 3)

TACTICS

Moving the fly slow and deep seems to score. As an angler of the

Midlands reservoirs, I've not often encountered the mayfly up here, and when I did, it turned a lot of my former ideas upside down.

It was the first day of June, and we visited Bishop's Bowl in Warwickshire for the first time. I gather that the hatches of mayfly can be long, drawn out and not particularly special at the Bowl. That wasn't the case on the day we visited.

At about 11 am, a steady stream of dark olive mayflies began to appear. We'd not seen *vulgata* before, and made a few mistakes before we cracked it. To begin with, the last thing the fish wanted was a creamy-coloured nymph. Whatever shade the *vulgata* nymph is, the trout wanted olive green nymphs. And as for grubbing them deep, we might as well have fished a bath tub. They wanted a very fast up to the surface retrieve, nothing like what I'd imagine from a creeping nymph. Meanwhile the insects continued to hatch in quite shallow water which was nothing like the deeps where the takes came!

As it was a guest day, we'd decided not to kill fish, and with a good stock in the water everyone was catching something. But having found the method, it was literally a fish a cast.

My only regret was that we didn't spoon a few more fish. The one we did kill and spoon had only adult mayflies in it. Since then I've read that one consistent regular on the water, John Macdonald, uses a fluorescent green Mayfly Nymph.

A WARNING

One thing worth noting with these big nymphs is that pulled fast they're all extremely good lures. In fact I once got a 6 lb 8 oz brown at the Andover (Hampshire) Rooksbury Mill fishery stripping a green Seal's Fur Nymph on a slow-sinking line. That was in sheer desperation in a flat calm and blazing sunshine.

As a consequence, I can't help feeling that a lot of the success of big nymphs comes when they're fished too fast on overstocked small waters. Stockies home in and grab them, the angler goes home with a full bag, and the fishery owner keeps happily to his 'nymph and dry fly' rule, secure in the knowledge that he has no lure strippers at his fishery. Wait until that angler comes back with a pink nymph and does the same!

THE TADPOLE – NYMPH OR LURE?

While on the subject of the borderline between nymph and lure, it seems as good a time as any to mention a fly that sits on the borderline. To put the Tadpole among non-specific imitators seems to take things too far. In many ways it's an out and out lure. But that said, it has a role to play for the nymph angler on several occasions.

First, a clarification: trout rarely feed on tadpoles as such, and when they do, it will nearly always be frog tadpoles, not toad tadpoles. 'Toadpoles' must have the vile taste of the adult, which is itself free from predation. If trout are feeding on tadpoles, however, my simple black version of this fly will undoubtedly catch.

As I'll mention later, when the trout are feeding on leeches it's the only fly you'll need. With its simple chenille body, and marabou tail it's almost a close copy of the natural.

Apart from these two beasties, it would be hard to build a case for the 'Taddie' as an imitative nymph pattern. In some guises, for instance black and green, orange, pink, white, white and blue, and yellow the Tadpole is simply a lure (the white being a superb fry pattern). But in black, brown, and olive, the nymph angler has three very deadly, very nymph-like patterns that can be fished with almost all the standard techniques. The fly is my castable version of the Dog Nobbler, the fly that has spawned as many lead-head variations as there are flydressers. My tadpole pattern is lightly leaded, on a standard shank hook, but has a tail barely the length of the body, giving plenty of action, but minimising short takes.

We all have days when we arrive at a water, perhaps a new venue, and find that there's no clue as to what the fish are feeding on. We have a couple of choices – we can try a Black Lure, or we can put our faith in a non-specific 'grubber' like a Zulu Nymph.

But more and more often I've found that my first choice exploring fly is a Tadpole. Put one on the point, with a Spider on the dropper, and you have all the advantages of a lure, but no need to fish anything but standard nymph tactics.

On a full-blooded reservoir, a black Tadpole is my first choice, with, in the early season a Black Spider on the dropper, and later in the year an Olive or Yellow Spider. On small waters a green or olive Tadpole on the point is a passable damsel or dragonfly nymph imitator. Alternatively a brown Tadpole covers most of the other large nymphs. On waters where *danica* mayfly are common, a creamy Tadpole (or at a pinch a white Tadpole) also makes a passable imitator.

Very often the Tadpole will quickly bring a fish to the bank. Then you can use the spoon to establish its feeding preference. It's extraordinary how the sinuous wiggle of that marabou tail will persuade a fish to take, even if its diet consists of tiny food forms.

So, is the Tadpole a nymph or a lure? Well, it's a deadly lure. The extraordinary results of the pink Tadpole, which takes everything from rainbow stockies to wild small stream browns, proves that more than adequately. But fished slowly and seductively the Tadpole could be considered a nymph, especially on waters where the 'big boys' – damsels, mayflies, dragonflies, alders, and large water beetle larvae – are common.

9 · SHRIMPS AND SNAILS – NOT ALL 'NYMPHS' HAVE SIX LEGS!

There are several aquatic creatures that seem to feature regularly on the trout's menu that are not nymphs in the sense that the entomologist would describe them.

Crustaceans like the shrimp and the freshwater louse; gastropods like the many varieties of snail; and leeches: none of these resemble any of the other underwater creatures, but they appear often enough to attract the imitative angler's attention, and as a consequence are usually grouped with the anglers' nymphs. While snails and leeches are found in most waters, and shrimp in all but the most acid waters, trout don't always feed on them. There does seem to be a stage when they come under heavy predation, but this doesn't always last long.

THE SHRIMP

Let's start with the shrimp. In the early days at newer reservoirs like Grafham and Rutland trout fed quite happily on shrimp. But as other food sources established themselves, or, perhaps, as the bottom and reservoir environment matured, trout moved off the shrimp onto other foods. I've found at the more mature Eye Brook, that, though the weed seethes with shrimp when I drag it up on my anchor, the trout rarely touch them. So rarely, that I've yet in 20 years to spoon one from an Eye Brook trout.

You can, however, fish the shrimp effectively near weedbeds, and in the lower layers of typical nymphing swims (ie. not too deep, with the odd weedbed), in a similar way to the *corixa*. Adapt the retrieves to fish much deeper and slower than the *corixa*, but still adopting the sink-and-draw that works with *corixa*. The shrimp is a short-burst-and-pause swimmer, flitting between the weedbeds, so don't fish it too steadily. A short draw, a long pause, a long draw then a short pause – mix up the speeds.

While it's usual to see an olive green shrimp, and on some waters or over different bottoms, a brown/olive shrimp, there has long been a controversy over the orange shrimps so often spooned from trout. It's now clear that a chemical change takes place in a shrimp when it dies, and it turns a pale orange. Thus any shrimp-feeding trout might contain at least a few orange shrimps, and a trout that has been on shrimp some time before, might contain all orange shrimps.

For many years it was suggested that orange shrimps were in mating colours. Certainly there do seem to be occasions when large numbers of shrimps die off at once, possibly after breeding, and it's the carotene in their bodies that turns them orange. Incidentally, the same chemical gives trout an even brighter pink flesh, and although trout get carotene from natural feeding, it is also fed to them in the cages when they're young. So beware of 'superb pink fleshed trout' in the small fishery adverts. Carotene, by the way, is also what turns flamingos pink.

What to do if your trout is full of dead shrimps? Well, he and others may still be taking the live shrimps, but on at least one occasion I came across trout grazing on the dead ones. It was at Rutland in around the second season: I was fishing Whitwell Creek before it was turned into an inland Skegness beach. It was a lovely warm afternoon, and before the breeze went, I'd picked up three nice fish. But the trout seemed to have gone with the wind.

Spooning the last fish I'd found an orange shrimp or two among the buzzers. So, without much hope, I tied one on the point, and pitched it out while I had a cup of tea. In the now flat calm, the line didn't even drift. But it did move after a few minutes, slowly drawing away towards the far bank. Lifting, I was fast into a super rainbow of 3 lb.

The spoon revealed more orange shrimp. I took two more trout that day. The only way to catch was to cast out a long line, put down the rod, and wait; retrieving the flies was a waste of time. Around 6 pm a cold wind finished my sport for the day.

There are two lessons here. One is that the correct presentation scored again, even though it was necessary to copy an unmoving shrimp, flat on the bottom. Incidentally, had there been a breeze, it would still have been possible to fish a slow-sinker and watch for takes. The second is that trout aren't always cruising in mid-water taking nymphs with a delicate suck. They like nothing better than a good grub in the weeds on occasions.

THE FRESHWATER LOUSE

A creature that turned up regularly in the fish caught over deep water at Rutland, Grafham and Draycote in the hey-day of lead lining was the freshwater or hog louse, a crustacean very like the shrimp. Similar to a wood louse in size and shape, it seems to fill a deep water niche, while the shrimp lives in the shallows. A useful imitation is a plump short shank Hare's Ear. One night, lazily trailing a floating line with a nymph on it, as I rowed back to the Eye Brook lodge, I picked up a trout over 40 feet of water: the 2 lb brown was stuffed with freshwater louse. That makes the pattern a must for the deep water nymphing we'll discuss later.

THE SNAIL

When grubbing around, trout are also happy to pick up snails. But how do we imitate something that moves every bit as slowly as its terrestrial counterpart? Well, there are no easy answers.

It's not at all uncommon to spoon a mass of weed and snails from a trout (and of course there's no way to imitate a snail sitting on a weed stalk!). Nor is it unusual for the deep water boat fishermen to haul up a big brown that nearly rattles with snails – which it will have picked up off the bottom, for sure. One solution is a Booby-style pattern fished static on a short leader and fast-sink line. Cork or deer hair can be used, and I dress a deer hair pattern for many of my customers. Unfortunately, it's very like a feed pellet.

Some species of snail indulge in what is usually called a migration: what they do is cling to the surface,shell down, and drift freely on the wind. The same buoyant patterns can be cast out on a floating line, and simply allowed to drift too.

Look out for these migrations in the autumn. Though they seem less

From top: Red Booby Nymph and Eye Brook Stick; claret Suspender Buzzer and longshank Hare's Ear;
Olive Shrimp and Baddow; Orange Shrimp.
Picture by Peter Hilton

From top: Longshank BP Nymph, Mayfly Nymph, Green Nymph, Green and Brown Nymph, Invicta Nymph, Zulu Nymph.
Picture by Peter Hilton

From top: Bloodworm and Buzzer Larva; BP Buzzer and Lime Buzzer; Cove Pheasant Tail and Fraser Nymph.
Picture by Peter Hilton

From top: Silver Corixa and olive Hare's Ear; dirty yellow Corixa and claret Hare's Ear; Greenwell's Spider and amber Sedge Pupa; brown Hackled Pheasant Tail and Hatching Sedge; ginger Hackled Pheasant Tail and Grey Duster Damp Dry.
Picture by Peter Hilton

common than in former years, I have had some marvellous sport at Grafham and Rutland in the past with a cork pattern. If caught without a cork pattern, a greased-up Black and Peacock may catch. A freak pattern that can also kill is a slowly retrieved orange Seal's Fur Nymph, just sub-surface.

Incidentally, trout feeding on the snails are very preoccupied. It pays to look out for snails if faced with thrashing fish everywhere and no sign of fly life on the water.

THE LEECH

Leeches, too, are often found on, and in, deep water fish. On other occasions they're plentiful in the shallows, too. In fact in the early days at Rutland and Grafham it was not uncommon to find your waders covered with the little suckers when you came out of the water. Trout do eat leeches, and though not common in spoonings, I've come across them in fish in newly-flooded lakes, and more recently in what was, I suppose, an especially hungry winter-caught rainbow from Rutland Water.

The best pattern for the leech is a standard Tadpole (a simple leaded fly with marabou tail, and chenille body), in brown or black. This fly is such an excellent lure though, that no one will believe you're nymphing!

THE WATER BEETLE

This is one other insect you may find in trout. I've only ever spooned them out of small water fish, so perhaps they are a last resort food. Faced with a spoon full of tiny dark beetles, though, a Black Spider or a Black and Peacock will usually do the trick.

10 · THE CAENIS – NO EASY SOLUTIONS

The questioner hopped up from his seat at the back of the room, and came out with the humdinger he'd been storing up all evening. 'What,' he asked, 'do you do in a *caenis* hatch?' 'Go to the pub,' I replied.

I don't do many club evenings, and perhaps that story illustrates why. I simply hadn't got an answer for the angler in question, and frankly he wasn't all that pleased. But when the little devils start hatching, I really do think very hard about throwing in the towel.

One of the Ephemeroptera, and therefore closely related to the large mayflies (and not dissimilar in appearance, though far, far smaller), this particular beastie is so minute, and appears in such numbers, that it's frequently known as the 'anglers' curse'. Curse, because it's seemingly impossible to create an artificial nymph or adult that will catch fish consistently, and because, of all the many foods that trout feed on, the *caenis* seems to induce total preoccupation. Trout mopping these up simply won't look at anything else.

It is almost impossible to describe a *caenis* hatch on the grand scale, and do it justice to someone who has never seen one. The little white devils get everywhere, up your nose, in your ears and hair. On occasions the whole surface of the water is covered with rising fish – and you can throw everything at them, and short of a hand grenade, you'll come away clean of fish.

The hatches can be short and sharp, and of an hour's duration, but try fishing soon after one, and you'll often find it just as hard. I have spent many evenings dressing up near-perfect copies of the *caenis* nymph only to have it completely ignored when it's cast right onto the nose of one of the many feeding trout. Short of your fly washing, with the others, straight into the fish's mouth, you have no chance. Of course, your fly is merely one white speck among what may be millions. So your best bet is to fish when a hatch starts, or when it begins to peter out. You may also catch on a *caenis* nymph when there's no hatch at all, and you may occasionally do quite well in a sparse hatch.

So what else can be done? If on the bank, I would try to get away from the main area of activity, and fish slow and deep with a good standard pattern like a Spider, or Buzzer. Just occasionally you'll find that some better fish are disdaining the yobbo riot at the surface, and feeding below; often these fish are handy browns. If there's deep water near the shore, work through this with a Booby nymph. Above all concentrate, and try to ignore the orgy of feeding on the surface. In the boat, do much the same, looking for water of 15 feet plus. Here you may find some fish feeding on buzzers or hog lice. Try to assume that not all the fish are on the top.

One July evening I took a boat out on Eye Brook, and down by my favourite spot, off the island, I took five nice fish on a yellow Hatching Sedge, as a trickle of the natural insects came off from about 6 pm, and the trout fed nicely. About 8 pm a few *caenis* appeared and I stopped catching. On this occasion, sick of breathing and eating the white snowstorm of insects (I can't say I share the trout's affection for the taste of *caenis*), I moved over deeper water. About 300 yards out, there was only a smattering of *caenis* on the water, and the odd fish showing. I anchored in 25 feet of water, and began to fish deep. By closing time I'd caught three more fish, one a very nice brown of 3 lb 6 oz, and all on the Hatching Sedge.

On another occasion I tried a yellow Booby Nymph stripped through the top, and took no less than seven fish. I could see fish come from yards away to take the fly, despite a heavy hatch of *caenis*. I really thought I'd cracked it, but unfortunately, it's never worked again when the *caenis* were about.

If you wish, try a lure on *caenis* feeders. Just occasionally it will bring you a fish or two. One of my fluorescent Pink Panthers was quite successful – just once! One final note – there are two main species of *caenis* that the angler may encounter, *caenis robusta* and *caenis horaria*. While such details may impress your mates in the pub, they will have been no use at all to you when faced by the rise that sent you *to* the pub. For all intents and purposes, both sub-species hatch at similar times and look virtually the same.

11 · NON-SPECIFIC IMITATORS – THE DEADLY ILLUSION

Virtually every fly that I use and recommend for nymphing comes into this category. Every one can be a deadly pattern on its day, and each one is proof of the wisdom of the saying we quoted earlier: it truly is not what you fish, but the way you fish it, that gets results. If we exclude the Buzzer Larvae, Bloodworm, and the Buzzer Pupae patterns; the Eye Brook Caddis, the Sedge Pupae, and the Hatching Sedge; my Mayfly Nymph; and the Corixa, virtually any of my other patterns can fall into this group.

There are a couple of points worth noting here before we get onto non-specific imitators. One is that all trout, but especially rainbows, get a large percentage of their nutrition from daphnia. These freshwater plankton form a rich soup through which the trout may cruise with their mouths open. We can't imitate daphnia effectively, so we have two choices – we can resort to stripping a lure and attracting the odd fish to a bright flash of pink or orange – or we can fish a nymph which in its unlikely size or colour may distract the trout from daphnia.

A classic pattern is the orange longshank Seal's Fur Nymph. Applying the techniques from Chapter 3, we'll take many fish with it, on days when fishing standard patterns might only produce the odd pull. A second point is that however perceptive a trout's eyesight may seem on occasions, basically trout are not very bright eating machines. The 'image' of food constantly attracts them. I would argue that fishing a nymphy profile of the right sort attracts them more than a lure, in fact it deceives them into taking, which is an altogether more satisfying style of fishing.

Most of the non-specific patterns are hard to match to a natural, and while others may talk of the success of their orange Damsel Nymph pattern, I prefer to make no specific claims, but to merely note that these flies all have the slim bodies, and delicate legs (in the shape of hackles or tips of the body materials) that make a trout think it is eating natural food. With the right retrieve – supplied by the angler – the hypnotizing trick is complete and the fish takes.

There are two types of non-specifics, which we might label 'possibles' and 'impossibles'. Possibles could actually be a natural insect of some type. Impossibles, usually due to their colour, or size, could never actually be closely related to any aquatic insect – yet the trout is fooled.

Let's start with possibles, and perhaps the best of these is the Spider series. There's nothing new about Spider patterns, and their virtues have been known for years, especially in the north of England. They were probably the predecessors of nymphs as we know them.

Let me quickly run through my series by colour, and relate each fly to a role. Black is pretty obvious: aside from the buzzer family, a number of other small black gnats and beetles find their way onto and into the water. This must rate as one of my very best killers. Brown, too, relates to the buzzers, to some beetles, and perhaps to some sedges and olives, and is a good early-season change of colour. Claret is a third early-season colour, and a good stand-by for some of the darker northern members of the olive family. Olive is the 'all things to all fish' colour of spring and summer. Buzzers, olives, sedges, and a host of terrestrial creatures are one or another shade of green. Orange is the colour I use for orange buzzers, and sedges, and is an excellent colour in a daphnia bloom or in coloured water. Finally, yellow with a Greenwell's hackle – really my version of the classic Greenwell's Spider – is a good fly in an olive hatch, and for some buzzers and sedges.

Next on my possibles list is the Baddow Special, an old favourite for Hanningfield anglers: it could well be seen as a caddis, though it is also a very good out-and-out lure. That probably has much to do with its bright fluorescent green tail, and extra long white hackle.

My most successful nymph thus far is the Fraser Nymph. I first dressed this as a large buff buzzer (as we'll see), but rapidly discovered that it killed in a hatch of olives, and on innumerable other occasions. There's something about the washed-out buff shade that seems irresistible to trout. The addition of green rib and olive thorax seems to change the whole colour of the fly. If it hadn't been for the advent of my BP series, I'd have no doubt tried other colours with success.

Much the same can be said of the Cove Nymph which again relies on profile, and something in the reddish brown and black mix of cock pheasant tail to deceive fish whatever they're feeding, or not feeding on.

Still on the pheasant tail theme, I can happily include my Hackled Pheasant Tails in among the possibles. It's entirely possible that the fish take them for buzzer, sedge, and especially olive, for *corixa*, an underwater beetle, or even a caddis.

Some of the longshank Seal's Fur Nymphs can be included as possibles, some not. Longshanks in all the buzzer shades will catch in a buzzer hatch – though it's rare to see a buzzer of such size. They score I believe in two ways: flat in the surface film they reflect the extra length of the natural buzzer crawling from its shuck; and, more fundamentally, they stand out in a crowd, as an extra large, extra tempting mouthful. Specific shades – brown, green and the brown-and-green – suggest or even copy a damsel nymph more than adequately. Again, the dark brown version may be taken at a pinch as an alder larva or caddis. A further role for the whole series is as a more than adequate stand-by for all those big nymph situations on any water. The new longshank BP series also fits all these requirements.

The Invicta Nymph is a useful pattern for a sedge hatch, resembling a sort of giant sedge pupa and, probably because of that, is good in a high summer daphnia bloom.

Then come the impossibles. It really is difficult to relate the largest of these, the Hare's Ear series, to any insect specifically. Suffice to say that they're very good as an olive or sedge pattern, quite good in an emergency to imitate a shrimp, passable in their longshank form as an alder larva, sometimes effective in a buzzer hatch, and even make a fair copy of a pellet! All of which seems impossible when you consider the spiky profile of a well-dressed Hare's Ear, including plenty of guard hairs which stick out at every angle. But in the water it must be a different story. Air bubbles must be trapped everywhere, and the fine strands must be constantly agitated in the water. I've now widened the range by blending the hare fur and getting a number of colours. In all of them it's excellent.

A pattern that actually resembles very little, is the Zulu Nymph, another pattern that has all the virtues of a deadly wet fly. With its large size, black body, and red tail it resembles no insect I can think of; but grubbed deep and slow in the early season, it's a killer. That flash of red has its own secret appeal. A recent development on the same theme has been my Dee Spider, dressed for the Welsh Dee browns and grayling, but with a proven record already on stillwater fish. Browns in particular seem to like the black and red combination – a combination found as far as I know only on above-water terrestrials like soldier beetles and heather flies. The Dee Spider too, has a red tail of hackle fibres – the rest being a black mole body, silver wire rib, and two turns of furnace hen. Pick a feather with a wide dark central band.

Finally the Booby Nymphs. Although visually impossible, with their huge beady 'eyes' of foam, they still seem to deceive fish. When the beads are large enough to support the fly, you'll find that no creature in British waters has such large eyes, so there's no place for the close-copy approach. Instead, we must ignore those great blobs, and go instead for a profile, and a colour that is simply 'nymphy'. And by now we all know the colours and styles that work. Then while we ignore those unlikely eyes, we may well be delighted to find that the trout do too.

Writing this, my thoughts go back constantly to a customer of mine who uses flies that are simple dubbings of sparse fur on the hook shank. He catches more good Rutland fish than almost anyone I've ever heard of. Once again we come back to the golden rule – the trout will have anything if it's fished properly – like a nymph.

12 · THE BOOBY SERIES – FAST-SINK LINE NYMPHING

While we mostly think of nymph fishing as a job best done with a floating line, and often in the top few feet of water, there are quite a few nymphy creatures that spend most of their lives in the lower layers, and plenty more that will spend long periods near the bottom when the weather conditions affect them. These conditions might be atmospheric pressure, a cold wind pushing icy water across the upper layers, or any wind that sweeps food along on a current and dips it down into the undertow.

Nymphs of bugs like damsels, alders, and even some of the free-swimming sedge pupae don't make a dramatic hatch at the water surface. Instead they crawl up from the lake bottom (or sometimes swim), climb up a weed stem, and shuck their nymphal skins in the open air. Caddis, too, creep about in the depths slowly.

All this means that trout, being the lazy creatures they are, and fond of the sheltered areas where food can be soaked up at will, will often sit in the bottom few inches, picking off some of these high-protein food forms. Being fussy, once they get into this habit, they'll often stick with it for long periods. At the same time, in the early colder days, though the trout may seek what is often warmer shallow water, they may still stay hard on the bottom in that water.

While we can effectively fish the bottom with floater or sink-tip line, there are occasions when presentation inches from the bottom is crucial, and in any case, fishing with a fast-sinking line will save us a lot of time. That's where the Booby Nymphs come in.

Booby Nymphs didn't start as bottom-grubbing flies, but grew out of the Suspender Buzzer series. For those that haven't seen these flies, they're a standard buzzer made buoyant by a single foam bead, wrapped in an old nylon stocking and tied to the head of the hook. The fly began life many years ago in the United States with a pattern called the Natant Nymph.

Discussions with former *Trout Fisherman* editor John Wilshaw led to the idea of dressing flies with more than one bead attached. A slow-sinking Hare's Ear had its uses and successes. Designed to be cast to cruising fish, it had an undersized bead at the head.

As a hatching nymph does not hang like a Suspender Buzzer does, tail down, but lies almost flat in the surface film, it was also possible to add beads to get this effect. A row of foam beads down the back of a Hare's Ear gave it a rather shrimp-like profile. That too was successful, but still needs some really good hatches to test it properly.

But, as it often does when experimenting at the vice, my mind strayed onto other variations. Two beads went on at the head of the longshank hook, and the Booby Nobbler was born. Strictly speaking it is outside the brief of this book, being little more than a reverse Dog Nobbler. Where the original fly was leaded to dive, and was then pulled up jerkily, my fly floated upwards of its own accord, then a pull on the line moved it downwards. And always, on a fast-sinking line, its effective fishing depth could be controlled.

What followed was well within the nymphing world. It immediately occurred to me that Suspender Buzzers could be used in this style, and with every chance of a really lifelike presentation. Put one on a 10 foot or so leader, allow it to sink, then bring the fly to the bottom with a couple of sharp pulls. Then nothing other than watching the line like a 'swingtip' for takes is required, as the fly makes its quite natural-seeming vertical passage towards the surface. As the natural unevenness of the seal's fur is built-in and the fly is dressed 'around the bend', the fly will wiggle a little as it floats up.

A successful alternative to this was developed by Bob and Steve Church, after Steve copied some 'overgrown' Booby Nobblers from a fishing friend's hat. These were very buoyant indeed, as were Steve's

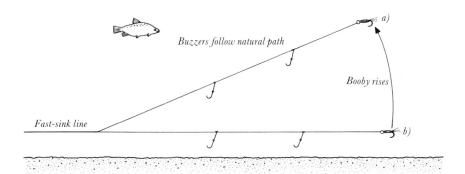

Fig 19

The dropper and Booby Nymph set up – fish with long pauses and short pulls. Swingtip to spot the takes

copies. Bob then added two droppers with nymphs on them. To fish them: cast out, pull to sink the point fly, then swingtip again, watching for long smooth pulls as the buzzers (or other pupae) are taken on the rise. Takes often come to the Booby Nobbler-type fly on the point, too. (An alternative is a simple lump of stocking-covered foam with a brown hackle. I'm afraid it looks a lot like a pellet, and I don't use it.) However, the longshank Booby nymphs, with their double bead heads, proved deadly both for me, and other anglers who mastered the technique of this unusual style.

The two beads were originally tried with the idea of pushing water at the surface – a similar but more buoyant idea than a palmered pattern, and less bulky than a muddler-headed one. A bonus when the fly was sunk was the turbulence set up by the beads. This gave extra action to the sinuous marabou tail of the Booby Nobblers, and to some extent the longshank nymphs. They proved their worth on cold early-season days, for winter fishing, and when big winds set up a current, and undertow. They also proved to take some slightly better fish. I suppose this is hardly surprising. If you were a big, fat, smart trout, would you race around after tiny buzzer pupae, which after all can swim a bit, and are always

Hooked deep in the water on a Booby Nymph this excellent rainbow shot to the surface, sounded, then leapt again.

drifting, or would you choose the easy life, grubbing about the bottom gobbling 2-inch-long damsels, alders and caddis – most of which are available with the minimum of effort?

Let's take a look at a standard Booby Nymph tackle set up. While nylon length can be adjusted to cope with a number of different retrieve speeds, my standard would be an unusually short level leader of 5 or 6 feet, needle knotted straight onto the fly line. I keep a fast-sink line specially set up for this style of fishing. The nylon leader I use is usually 6-8 lb. On the occasions when it is necessary to use a lighter line it is best to attach a small tippet of about 12 inches, but for this unusual style of nymphing it is vital to keep the number of knots to a minimum: any knots will pick up weed and slime from the bottom, making the leader visible. You will of course need a longer leader for standard lure fishing.

Suitable patterns are longshank Hare's Ear (for alders, caddis, and maybe damsels), longshank red Seal's Fur, my favourite (deadly as a bloodworm pattern), and olive Seal's Fur (for damsels). A black Seal's Fur pattern is a useful allrounder. But although those are the main colours, it's amazing just what will produce results consistently. One of my customers from Louth in Lincolnshire, Alan Clapp, is a regular at Toft Newton, Gerald Denton's excellently run concrete bowl fishery near Market Rasen.

He tells me that he's found that a yellow Booby Nymph can be lethal fished slowly up the corrugated walls of this reservoir. One of his outstanding performances was an end-of-season double limit, while other anglers struggled. He fishes the Booby Nymph incredibly slowly: one cast can take 10 minutes to fish out. And as an inveterate experimenter he's found that on some easy days he can go as short as a 12 inch leader. Perhaps it's the slow retrieve, or the camouflage of the dark bottom, but sinking fly lines in this role just don't seem to scare fish.

We've already mentioned techniques in Chapter 3. What we must concentrate on here, is the speed of our retrieve, matched to the buoyancy of the fly, strength of undertow and the length of the leader. A dead-slow steady retrieve will give the longshank patterns a smooth swim just a foot or so off the bottom. A series of pulls and pauses will give the fly a tempting sink-and-draw action – this style is often the deadliest of all. At a pinch, especially when a powerful wind is setting up an undertow, we can simply slide the line out on the current, and hold on, again swingtipping for takes. The underwater currents supply the motion.

There was one never-to-be-forgotten April evening when we first came up with the Booby series. I arrived optimistically at the Eye Brook, only to find a howling gale blowing from the north west, so strong that the boats had been called in. I had intended to do a bit of rough shore nymphing from a boat, but with that option gone, I was obviously going to be confined to the bank. However, I'd not got my waders with me, so it had to be the dam.

This was not the disaster it might have been. Here was an opportunity to try out something we thought would work, but so far hadn't seen such excellent conditions for testing. On the far side of the dam at Harrison's Corner, the waves were crashing onto the dam, with what must have been a warmer surface layer turning back into a very powerful undertow. Time then, for a bit of undertow nymphing. The tackle was a

Fig 20

Swingtipping the Booby into a head wind: movements of the fly line can clearly indicate fishy interest

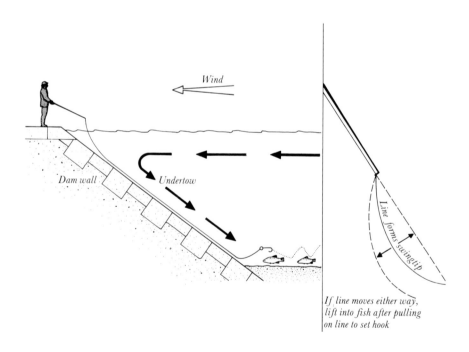

weight-forward fast-sinking lead-preg, with a longer-than-usual, straight leader of 10 feet, with no knots.

The strong undertow was going to drag the fly down, unquestionably, so I opted for the slightly longer leader that would keep the fly bouncing about just a foot or so off the bottom. The fly was a red Booby Nymph.

Casting was interesting. Facing straight into the wind, I eventually had to wait for a lull in the wind before casting about 40 feet. Incidentally, the very short Booby leaders are ideal when punching into a wind – even the knot-free construction helps to avoid tangles.

With the whole dam to myself, I settled down well back from the water, and just let the whole lot slide down into the depths. The undertow dragged out far more line than I could ever have cast. The line felt very heavy as it slid into the depths. Eventually it settled on the bottom. All I had to do now was hold on. It took only 10 minutes to prove that what we thought would work, did. The line suddenly went light, and a quick pull with my left hand, then a lift of the rod, brought a super pound-and-a-half brown trout to the net. The spoon showed that it had quietly been eating anything and everything that floated along to it on the undertow – red and green larvae; caddis; a few buzzer pupae; bits of weed and twigs; and the odd small fry swept away by the current.

I made just seven casts that evening, landed six nice trout, and lost another brute that ran out the whole fly line, and a lot of backing. (I'm pretty sure that was one of Eye Brook's monster carp!) Down on the comfortable sheltered shore several other bank anglers who had no intention of braving the hard fishing into the wind caught virtually nothing.

Indeed, if we're due for a lunch break it's always worth pitching out a buoyant pattern on a short leader and leaving it to fish for itself. There's nearly always a little current to move it about, I suspect, and trout really will often pick up the right static pattern.

On snag-ridden bottoms, the line may well slide through, but a hook will hang up. Fishing the fly on a longer leader, slowly and smoothly, should keep it clear of the snags. Hit takes this way: hold the line straight from the butt ring (don't thread it over your right index finger), in your left hand, and strike by pulling with the hand, not by lifting the rod.

One of the ultimate places to try the tactic is on the concrete bowls like Datchet, Toft Newton, or Farmoor, where flies very often need to be

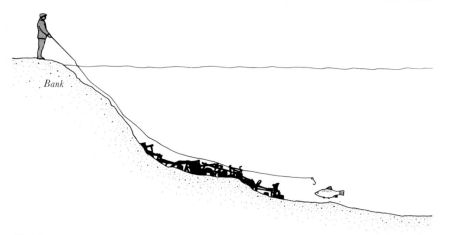

Fig 21

A Booby can be carefully and slowly worked over sunken obstructions

eased along hard against the concrete, and often quite deep. Of course, patterns like Dick Walker's Dambuster have been used for years to creep up a dam, bouncing along on their long hackles, and other buoyant lure patterns designed by Walker, and latterly Mike Peters, have also been successful in this role. But the Booby Nymphs are another string to the nymph angler's bow, allowing him a lifelike presentation, and a few tricks that can't be achieved any other way.

112

13 · THE DRIFTING BOAT – A NEW AREA FOR THE NYMPH ANGLER

The biggest boom in our sport in the 80s has been the renewed interest in loch-style, traditional, or over-the-front fishing. Always performed from a broadside drifting boat, it has become the great equaliser for competition fishing. In the past, I've been known for criticising the mindless traditionalism of many over-the-front anglers. My criticism has mainly been based on the Eye Brook traditionalists, who'll drift over open, deep, and barren water, shortlining with floaters in even the coldest months.

As the Eye Brook rules allow trolling, but only between drifts, so many of these anglers have come to rely on long zig-zag journeys back up to the next drift, lines trailing behind their electric motor powered boats. Trolling, in case anyone doesn't know, is the deadliest and most boring method of hooking trout – which is why it's banned at most waters.

Until the last few seasons, over-the-front anglers relied mainly on wet flies of the most traditional sort. Such flies as Dunkelds, Wickham's Fancies, and Soldier Palmers bear no resemblance to any living fly (which is not to say that fished in a deceitful fashion, they won't be taken by nymph-feeding fish). But, led by the skilled anglers of the Bristol reservoirs, a rapid change is coming over the traditional boating scene. It's now increasingly clear that an all-nymph cast, or nymph and wet fly mixed, will catch even more fish.

This is something I've always known, but without the impetus of an

113

interest in competition fishing to get me into a drifting boat, it's often been easier to fish at anchor. Competition fishing, however, is here to stay. Some of the International restrictions interfere with the normal nymphing styles, as we'll discuss later, but the record of men like England International Chris Ogborne, in both those Internationals and the Benson and Hedges, speaks for itself. Chris apparently fishes mostly nymphs over the front.

In addition, once the water warms from mid-May onwards, there are few more pleasurable ways of harvesting the moving shoals of fish. Casting is easy with the wind behind, and with a drifting boat slowly covering the water, you can also note 'hot spots', and explore new areas relatively quickly. One area springs to mind – there can be few experiences more enjoyable than just drifting across the shallows at the bottom of Rutland's South Arm, under the scenic Lax Hill, the weeds rich beneath the boat, and the shoals of rainbows sliding down the wind to meet you.

WHEN TO DRIFT

Perfect conditions for drifting are those that make the best nymphing days – overcast, with just enough wind to push you gently along, and just a few insects hatching steadily. In these conditions a lot of nymphs will be hatching and moving in the top few inches.

Of course, you can't always choose the conditions for a match. In a really big rolling wave it may well be the big hackled wet flies that come into their own. The nymph will score too, but you'll feel out of touch trying to move the flies slowly and intelligently in front of the boat. At the other extreme, some spectacular results have been achieved by the Bristol anglers in virtual flat calms with the nymph, and very fine tackle. In fact the nymph is categorically your best choice in such conditions, along with a Damp Dry pitched to showing fish. It was that type of tactic that won Bristol Reservoirs Flyfishers the Benson and Hedges title in a flat calm at Bewl Water in 1985 and at Grafham in 1986.

TACKLING UP

In ideal conditions, we can actually speed up our catch rate by going *to* the fish, not waiting for them to come to us. So before we slip the anchor, what sort of tackle set up should we go for?

I certainly don't feel the need for very long rods for this style, unlike some traditionalists. However, I might conceivably change over to my 10 footer, which I might couple with a DT 7 floater. The extra few inches can come in handy when completing a cast, and just holding the flies in the top few inches of water. Very long casts are not too necessary, but good presentation can be, hence the choice of a double taper line, which can be put down more delicately at short range. We could well want to hit a rising fish accurately with the flies. This is one reason why I make an exception and use three flies for this method. With a 15 foot, two dropper leader you can flank a fish with your nymphs more easily, showing him at least one.

At the same time, I like to have a top dropper fly that makes the traditional bulge or wake at the surface in front of the other nymphs. As most good traditional anglers appreciate, the main reason that the final dibble of the flies is so deadly is that it mimics perfectly that moment of hatching that most aquatic nymphs pause for at the surface. The trout are often persuaded that that pause is their last and easiest chance of a snack. (In fact every cast and retrieve should have that dibble at the end of it – a huge number of trout are caught at that moment whatever the method, from lure to nymph.)

Choice of fly depends on the time of the year, and whatever is around on the surface or in the fish. The top dropper will be a palmered fly, Booby Nymph or possibly a Suspender Buzzer. Below it there will usually be a Fraser Nymph (first choice from May to September), a longshank BP Nymph, longshank Seal's Fur, a Spider or Hackled Pheasant Tail, or a Hatching Sedge.

It's been my experience that my Buzzers fish better in a stationary boat, although they too have their days. But sedges and olives with their turn of speed in the water are a natural choice. However slow the drift, you have to keep the line moving, and it's easy to pull too fast. So perhaps Buzzer presentation is not easy to achieve. That said, on very calm days, I've cast out a Damp Dry, and had quite a few fish just drifting along, retrieving just fast enough to stay in touch.

In shallow water near weed beds, a Corixa can be productive, fished in a series of pulls and pauses.

TACTICS ON THE DRIFT

With just enough wind to push the boat gently along, a cast straight down the wind is easily made. Let the flies settle for a few seconds, then commence a retrieve that either just stays in touch with the flies, or brings them back just faster than the speed of the boat. As always, mix up figure-of-eight retrieves with slow steady draws. As we've already noted in the olives chapter, it can even pay to pitch at a fish, straighten the leader, then do nothing but watch the line.

In a faster drifting boat, you can find yourself stripping quite hard just to stay in touch. Many's the angler who has been accused of stripping in a cast like a madman, when in fact his fast retrieve leaves the actual flies hardly moving in the water, as the boat approaches from the other direction. But with your arm going like a fiddler's elbow, it's easy to lose a taking fish, or even snap the leader on a solid take, and far harder to judge the speed of the flies. A very fast strip that is genuinely moving the flies quickly means that we're turning our flies into lures, which defeats the purpose of fishing nymphs, and is better done with wet flies anyway.

The solution to the fast-drifting boat is a drogue, fitted as standard on some boats, easily borrowed from the lodge at other fisheries, and cheap to buy or make. It is generally a large square of strong cloth, usually with a central hole to let water through and hold the drogue fairly steady. Positioning in the boat is important – both ends of the boat should be level down the wind. Some experts even carry more than one size to control the speed of drift. On other waters, like Eye Brook, the lump-of-concrete-on-a-rope type of anchor – though quite useless *as* an anchor – makes a good drift controller in a strong breeze!

If the surface retrieve fails, and there are no fish, or very few, showing, it's time to get down a little deeper with a leaded pattern on the point, and perhaps remove the buoyant fly from the top dropper.

Replace it with a longshank Seal's Fur Nymph, in a bright colour like claret or orange. Then despite the loss of wake, the top dropper, with its eye-catching brightness, can still draw fish up to look at the flies. More on this in a moment. Slow the boat down a little with a drogue (or even two) as well, which will allow you a slower retrieve, and more sinking time. I remember a day when flies made all the difference, but there are so many lessons to be learnt from that story that we'll save it for later. Another day's sport tells much the same story, so let's look at that one.

The two anglers in question were an expert loch-style angler, and a novice, teamed together on a dour day at Patshull Park. They were fishing a pairs contest, and had missed out on the 'hot spots' when the boats left the dock. Patshull fish often sit in tight little shoals around the edges – a couple of boats had got over the shoals and were murdering the fish. The others struggled.

The two anglers in question had one fish to show by lunch, caught first thing by the novice on a Dog Nobbler. Then the novice got a couple more side-casting while the other rowed back up the wind. Exasperated, the loch-style expert set up for a drift broadside – unheard of on a small water like Patshull. On the first drift the expert moved fish, but didn't hook any. The novice tackled up, guessing at a suitable team, and proceeded to take nine fish while the expert rose them everywhere, and hooked one!

The difference? Well, in his haste the novice angler had put a leaded Hare's Ear on the middle dropper, and, quite obviously something in the angle, depth of retrieve, or in the curve of the final lift off (when many of the fish came), was helpfully affected by the lead.

Another lesson here – stationary nymphing wouldn't score that day – nor a lure from an anchored boat – but nearly all the trout caught took the Hare's Ear Nymph from the drifting boat. So it's always worth a try even on the most unlikely venue. Just for the record they finished third that day, worth a prize in Patshull's generous matches.

Of course you can fish deeper with a sink-tip or sinker, but somehow these don't seem to give the same effective presentation as a floater. I never use anything but floaters to fish this way. Once the fish appear to be more than 6 or 7 feet down, it's time to anchor up and use a sink-tip, or a slow retrieve with a leaded point fly.

NYMPHS AND WETS

I've lost count of the number of times that, as I've begun the process of holding each fly in turn in the surface film, a trout has moved up to the top dropper, swirled, missed or rejected the fly, and turned down. A fraction of a second later the leader snakes away, and the fish has just taken a fly lower down the cast. Just occasionally, for that reason, it will hugely improve your results to add a traditional wet fly on the top dropper.

Before giving up drifting and concluding that the fish are too deep, try something like a Dunkeld or Butcher on the top dropper. This will often bring fish up for a look from deeper water, and though they won't necessarily take the fly, they'll often have one of the more imitative nymphs behind it. The best times to try this are when a chill wind cools the surface, or when a fading sun turns the light very brassy.

Here we're talking about the classic wet fly inducement, with the true deceptiveness of the nymphs to back up the attractiveness of the top dropper wet fly. The old-time traditionalists know all about this, but having drawn up the fish, they have to rely on less-imitative patterns to actually hook him.

It was the advice of one of these traditionalists, heard at the Eye Brook, that brought me a good catch back in 1978 at Pitsford Water. It was a July evening, and near the Causeway a nice ripple had produced a couple of fish for me as I drifted slowly along casting an amber Sedge Pupa.

By 9 pm the wind was dying away, and sedges began to come off regularly, with for the first time that evening, plenty of fish showing on the top. The ripple was rapidly disappearing. My next few casts with the two amber Sedge Pupae, and a simple brown Palmer on the top dropper produced bumps and knocks, but no fish.

The sun got lower and lower in a clear sky, and I had to screw my eyes up to concentrate on the line. Remembering the advice of the Eye Brook veteran to fish gold flies in brassy light, I tied the next best thing, a Jersey Herd, on the point. This produced an immediate fish to the Jersey Herd which promptly fell off, and there was nothing for the next 20 minutes. I moved the flasher fly up to the top dropper, and put another amber Sedge Pupa on the point. At the second cast, a steady draw produced a nice rainbow, with the point fly in its mouth. It was closely followed by four more. When gutted, they were all stuffed with sedges. Yet without the allure of that Jersey Herd, they wouldn't look at my imitations.

Since then, when rapidly sorting through the box for a late fish or two, a Dunkeld or Jersey Herd on the top dropper has had exactly the same effect, and not just from a boat, either.

DAMP DRY TACTICS

When all goes flat, both on the lake and in the fishing, there are frequently a few fish sidling along on whatever breeze there is, taking the flies glued in the sticky surface film, that have failed to hatch. This is an ideal time to slip the anchor, and go off in search of them, casting a team of Damp Dries, just staying in touch. When a fish rises, don't strike at it, or even hurriedly lift. Watch for the line or leader to draw away – which it invariably will. If the fish has missed the fly, and simply swamped it, you'll then get another chance as he returns to look at it again. If you whip it away, he can't! It can pay to bring in the line very, very slowly in a figure-of-eight, feeling and watching for the fish.

Another method is to fish the flies in smooth short draws, imitating in classic wake fly style the adult trying to get off the water, or twitches, imitating the struggles of a nymph trying to shed its shuck. When a lot of fish are showing, this type of fishing is a real test of your coolness, and not for the faint-hearted.

SOLVING THE COMPETITION PROBLEMS

The rules of International drift fishing, intended to do away with out-and-out lure fishing, can affect the nymph angler. Flies must not be too large, only a fraction more than half an inch long, and must not have overlong tails. But nearly all my nymphs do, or can be dressed to fit inside this ideal.

While there's no restriction on foam buoyancy, you may not lead your flies in these competitions. Two ways to slightly overcome this problem are the use of heavy wire patterns; or to dress nymphs on double hooks. A standard shank salmon double can be within the rules for instance, and there's a lot of heavy metal in one of those.

You may also find yourself unable to use a drogue where it is not standard equipment on the boat, and if you have to move the flies extra fast, you may well do better with standard wet flies to lure the fish.

WET FLY VERSUS NYMPH

Over-the-front drifting has seen such a revival in recent years, that I couldn't have imagined writing this comparatively lengthy chapter in the early 80s. But as match fishing plays a bigger and bigger part in the modern sport, I still maintain that the nymph has a major part to play for those anglers who realise that it is deadly fished over-the-front. One final story to illustrate my confidence – just imagine if the first half of this story had taken place during a match where there was no limit, and where I *might* have been less inclined to help my boat partner.

I went out on Rutland one evening, with a traditionalist fanatic from Eye Brook. So keen is he on over-the-front that I decided to go along with him, though I'd have preferred fishing at anchor in a quiet bay. We went up the North Arm to the point there the old road sinks into the lake from the Hambleton Peninsula.

He set up a team of wet flies, while I put on two Fraser Nymphs, size 12, and a compromise Yellow Palmer on the top. In a gentle breeze I was well able to keep in touch with my flies, and on the first drift across I took six fish and missed several takes. My partner took just one fish on an Invicta.

Halfway through the next drift I had completed my limit, all the fish having taken a Fraser Nymph fished steadily just sub-surface, the Palmer making a wake. Few fish had shown on the top on both drifts, but despite that, they wanted the nymphs high in the water.

My partner was justifiably annoyed. After all, he is very expert at over-the-front fishing. I packed my rod away, and acted as boatman. By now my companion had tried about 20 different flies already, and several times declined my offer of a Fraser Nymph. As often happens, the more frustrated he got, the faster he began to retrieve the team of flies. I suggested a slower retrieve, but he remained convinced that wet flies worked better pulled fast. The trout didn't agree. In the end he accepted a Fraser Nymph, and slowed down a little. Second cast brought him a trout, and quite quickly he took a limit. On the way back he promised to give the nymph an extended try.

My son Shaun was so impressed with our results that he suggested an evening boat to try again, and on the next day, and in identical conditions, we set off down the North Arm to fish the same area.

I expected the same results with flies fished up in the surface, and the Brown Palmer just waking nicely. But well into the first drift we hadn't touched a fish. Shaun was already a bit peeved, and as he turned to ask me where all the fish were, he got into a really bad three fly tangle (another reason why I so often use just two flies!), and had no choice but to tackle up again.

On his fourth cast after starting again, he hooked a fish, which took, he told me, a Fraser Nymph. Two drifts later Shaun had six fish in the boat to my one, my only take, and on the next drift Shaun missed several fish and took two to complete a limit.

Setting up for a new drift I asked if all the fish had taken the Fraser Nymph. No, he said, some had had the Hare's Ear – *the leaded Hare's Ear* on the point. All along since the tangle, his flies had been fishing a few inches deeper than mine, and as so often happens, the fish had changed their habits, and that's where they now wanted it.

I changed flies, but only managed a couple of fish before the day ended. The same old lesson applies – it never pays to assume that fish are at the same depth, and it's always worth experimenting.

OTHER DRIFTING METHODS

If it pays to drift your flies around on the wind from the bank, we can get the same deadly presentation, bringing the flies across the trouts' noses by side-casting Northampton lure-style (where the boat is allowed to drift, bows first down the wind, and flies cast at right angles to the boat), from a boat drogued by the stern. A steady figure-of-eight is the best retrieve to try, or a series of slow steady draws.

In the big winds and perfect fly conditions of 1985's season, a really large Muddler with a nymph behind worked superbly: as the large, easily-seen fly drew up the fish, and the favourite patterns were longshank nymphs, it was hard to say if the successful anglers were nymphing or lure fishing.

14 · A CALENDAR FOR THE NYMPH ANGLER

MARCH/APRIL

At one time 1 April was the traditional start of the season, but with the growth of winter fishing and the virtual end of a close season anywhere for rainbows, the season now effectively starts in many places in March. In the mid-80s, however, we've struck a weather pattern that brings everything later and later, and is of paramount importance to the nymph angler. At one time we would have confidently expected a spell of warmer weather some time before the end of April, a steady rise in water temperature, and the beginnings of some nymph activity with fish showing on the surface. Instead we have experienced icy spells in February and March, and the type of vicious weather that has slowed down the normal processes to the extent that even May will see little trout movement from the bottom.

In addition, some vast waters like Rutland and Kielder cool down, and unfortunately warm up again so slowly that what was a steady progression of the seasons, honoured from year to year on the smaller waters, is practically irrelevant on the vast ones. Wisely, Kielder doesn't even open until June: I can see a useful argument for Rutland doing the same. Luckily smaller and shallower waters, from the tiny Wellingborough water Ringstead, to my beloved Eye Brook, behave a little more consistently – temperatures permitting, of course.

Bearing all this in mind, let's draw up some loose guidelines for March and April.

In March, and through most of April, weed will be pretty nearly non-existent, although there'll be some bottom weed, and possibly some terrestrial grass covered by high water levels just peeking through the surface. Also, perhaps, some long-dead flooded bankside weeds, and the rotting remnants of last year's aquatic weeds.

It pays to do two things – one is to recall where last year's heavy weed growths lay, and to fish those areas. The other is to make full use of any underwater structure that might shelter trout food, like old fences, trees, bushes and sunken brush. On some occasions the flooded bankside might also produce fish, sometimes in just a few inches of water. The colour of the water will vary from rather clear, to very dirty, in floods and high winds. But fish are unlikely to be too line shy at first, even in the clear water, so there's no need to fish too light a nylon point.

Very early in the season, fish can be found in some alarmingly shallow water. An April press day at Grafham found shoaling stockie rainbows hard on the bottom in two feet of water: this is because the shallows heat up more quickly than the deeps, and it's always worth investigating them. But for better fish, I generally look for water of 12 to 15 feet. Places to avoid are gravelly bottoms, creek mouths, and, except in the exceptional circumstances outlined, shallows, as here gather the black and out-of-condition rainbows, which despite the advent of genetically engineered female and triploid fish are still far too common on the big waters.

When to fish is another question. The warmest part of the day is the best choice – early morning starts are for the sparrows at this time of the year. Any fishy activity will reach a peak from mid-morning to mid-afternoon, even if it doesn't actually constitute a rise, and there are no fish to be seen on the surface.

It's important to remember my early-season advice on the buzzer in Chapter 4. Take note of the prevailing winds, and the wind on the day. Remember to face into warmer winds, and to get cold ones on your back.

So what can we expect in the way of nymphs and other bugs on the trout fishing menu? Possibly top of the list comes the caddis. Like a great many other immature aquatic insects it spends much of its time deep in the water, moving slowly, and keeping close to cover. In the dead weed-beds with him will be the immature alder nymphs, small, still-to-grow

123

damsel nymphs, snails, and shrimps. Over muddy bottoms the blood-worm will be common, as will some species of snails. Deep-grubbing fish will happily pick up snails and a bellyful of mud. Tiny red and green bloodworms will also turn up in spoonings, swept from the mud too. Our March and early April sessions, therefore, will often mean leaded flies or a sink-tip grubbing flies deep.

As the water warms into mid-April there may be a smattering of unusually small, and always dark buzzer pupae. In April look for black, brown, and dark olive to be the most usual colours. Some olive nymphs will appear late in the month, small and dark initially, and a Cove Nymph is more likely to score now than the paler Fraser Nymph.

Right at the end of April look out for the rather beautiful bottle green buzzer, a bright dark green colour. Also in early spoonings – probably because there's a limited amount of cover, making their minute forms visible, and a limited amount of food, making their pursuit worthwhile, despite the tiny amount of food they offer – is the red mite. Like its terrestrial cousin found on warm stones in the summer, this is a speck of red fringed with legs, and as I've said elsewhere, too small to imitate effectively.

Watch out too, for terrestrials, which seem to get going in numbers before their aquatic opposites. Beetles will regularly appear on the water at this time, and trout feeding on them should not be confused with fish rising to buzzers. By the end of April, in all but the coldest, deepest, and largest fisheries, the water has warmed sufficiently for both insect and fishy life to begin to liven up. And we are approaching May – in a warm year, one of the best months in the season.

MAY

These days you can guarantee just one thing about May: it will be a better nymphing month than April. At one time it was the certain start of the best nymphing period of the year, but a series of icy springs in the early 80s has changed the pattern of fishing, and it may well be early June before we see a really good rise on the Midland waters. Further south, the angler may well find superb nymphing this month, and, strangely, further north, where the trout are hardier – or so hungry that they feed avidly on even the smallest hatch.

The small waters will respond quickly to a warm spell, and can quickly get as much as a month ahead of their larger brethren. Waters like the Eye Brook which are shallower than some, will steal a fortnight from the Rutlands and Grafhams. Remember though, that, for the same reason, such waters are more quickly affected by adverse weather – sudden cold snaps, or long warm spells.

This is the month when the first weed appears poking its head out of the water, and the first mats of greeny cotton wool start to float up to the surface. Trout will now feed through the day on occasions, and not just by grubbing around deep. They'll move higher in the water to feed, and take buzzer pupae at all stages of their hatch.

Trout are busy this month, but not yet always cruising in open water. They can come to various drifting techniques, but mainly in water of 12 to 15 feet, not out over the deeps. The best nymphing spots are still near the weedbeds, and except in extraordinary weather conditions it's often possible to fish with the wind on your back. Small waters can be difficult now, as the fish have been fished exhaustively and seen everything. Of course, there are usually injections of fresh stockies – but they really have no idea what a nymph is, and are mostly caught before they find out.

To catch the better or overwintered smallwater fish is quite a challenge, then. Light tackle, down to 4 lb leaders is one advantage; another is to fish the difficult spots which other anglers have ignored. Most of all don't neglect the margins of small fisheries – try casting while standing back from the edge; or try casting *along* the edge. Good fish often shelter in close under the bank. Your other weapon is of course good nymphing technique which will sort out the fish other techniques miss! Even wise smallwater fish have to eat, and however aware they may be that orange lures offer little nourishment, they have to eat nymphs, and your fly could be on the menu.

What does that menu consist of this month? Well, on the large waters the olives arrive in good numbers, including some large ones I've heard confused with mayflies. The buzzers are now around in a huge range of colours, so the spoon is vital in a buzzer hatch. Size can be important too: there is a very large range of buzzer sizes. But don't forget that the freakishly large imitation can draw the fish to your fly out of a large hatch of the naturals.

Small damsel nymphs are present now, eating and growing towards the time at the end of the month when they'll climb up the weeds to hatch. Alders are already migrating to the bank to hatch, and you should not be fooled by the dark brown to black adults into thinking that sedges have already appeared – though later in May there may be just a sprinkling of small sedges.

Fish will also be feeding on daphnia now (and for most of the remaining season). This freshwater plankton will be lying deep in the water at first, and far from the surface daphnia tactics of later in the year, slow and deep will usually catch fish that turn out to have a mixed spooning of daphnia and buzzers in them.

With all this activity the *corixa*, shrimp, and snail, move further down the diet sheet. Terrestrials, though, move a notch or two up, and it's particularly important to look out for falls of hawthorn flies at this time. As this terrestrial sinks into the surface when it falls on the water, don't confuse a rise for a hawthorn for a rise to a still-born or hatching buzzer.

JUNE

Finally we've arrived! This is *the* month for the nymph angler. Take a fortnight's holiday, and book your place on the bank! Even the mighty Rutland Water is up at an acceptable temperature and the fish are on the top and moving down the wind everywhere.

As I've mentioned before, I always find it interesting that Kielder Water doesn't even open until June. Financial restraints stop this happening at Rutland Water, and other large fisheries – but what superb sport, and superb fish, would be the result if they all adopted this practice! Far from the tailless black monsters of the early season bank thrash, we would all take prime fit browns and rainbows right from the start, to whatever tactics we wished.

The weed grows rapidly this month, and a week or two away from the water can find you returning in search of a favourite spot that's no longer there – which only goes to emphasise the importance of intelligent weed cutting by the management on the best and most fertile waters. In the past there have been regular and unholy rows at Rutland, Bewl Water, and even on the Bristol reservoirs, as whole stretches of bank have been unfishable by high summer. The bank man not unnaturally expects his access to be as good as the boat angler. Of course the boat angler can use these conditions to his advantage, always being able to anchor up and fish the weedbeds effectively.

The trout will now move everywhere from right in the heart of the weed, to cruising out over deep water – not surprisingly really as there's food everywhere. In fact the only drawback is that, like humans, trout don't stuff all the time – even though to build up a bellyful of food they may have to cruise for long periods just browsing. So there may be periods through the day when they're uncatchable. This doesn't matter too much, because except on impossibly warm and bright days, you can almost guarantee that fish will be caught at some stage during the day. Moreover every nymphing technique may work at some stage, from a deeply-grubbed Bloodworm through to a waking Booby Nymph slid through the waves.

Small waters are a different proposition, especially if the weather warms up, and stays that way. Daytime sessions can be miserable, and progressively the fish will be catchable only first thing and last thing. If you're forced to fish the day through, your best bet may be the unmissable meal of a Damp Dry just cast out and left to drift – it's amazing how a good trout will fin up from the depths, 10 feet or more, to take the morsel glued in the surface film. The alternative is to go down to him with something like a red Booby Nymph grubbed deep on a leader just long enough to fish over the bottom weed, if any. Until the small waters cool again in September, these will be your standby techniques when all else fails.

The water on all fisheries will be either gin clear now, or tinged with the green of daphnia. Don't be put off by a green tinge. The fish still find our flies with consummate ease, although it can pay to use bright colours. In a daphnia bloom it's orange Seal's Fur Nymph time, of course. Overall a touch of colour in the water will definitely improve sport.

We welcome the real sedge hatches this month, most particularly as the light fades. Some memorable nights will see fish rising everywhere to the extent of nudging your waders. Catching them is another problem!

Early morning is the preserve of the buzzers, and some really big beasties appear now, with, just to confuse the issue, the tiny, bright, almost fluorescent lime buzzer that is so common in fish spoonings from Midland reservoir trout. This also arrives in a washed out yellow. Best imitated on a 22 hook, it calls for compromise, and this is about the only time I'll use a size 16 hook regularly, with a lime buzzer dressed to it. As far as other buzzers go, it's important to look for bloodworm higher in the water, either brought up on rising mats of weed, or looking for oxygenated higher layers as evening approaches.

Olives tend to peter out this month, even if they're very much still around in tiny but regular quantities, often mixed into the buzzer hatches.

The worst feature of this otherwise wonderful month is the arrival of the angler's curse, the snowstorm of little white *caenis*. I wish I had a pound for every promising evening they've ruined for me!

On small waters and some big ones like Tittesworth the mayfly has its 'duffer's fortnight' this month. With the changing seasons it became clear in the early 80s that this insect would be better named the 'junefly' now. Whether years ago the insect hatched in mid-May I don't know, but what is certain, is that they are now far more common in June than May.

Damsels start to move to the weeds and climb up out of the water to hatch. On some large waters, and on some very small ones, they do this in vast numbers, and even the adult is pursued by leaping fish as it hovers over or on the water. Certainly it offers a superb chance for some nice easy fishing with a good solid reliable size 10 longshank hook that is unlikely to lose your fish; and a comfortably quick retrieve, to match the natural's swimming, is easy to produce.

The big nymphs of damsel and mayfly provide excellent alternatives on the small water to the Booby methods, grubbed leaded and deep on a floater or even a sink-tip line.

JULY

This can be a copy of June, or it can be the worst month in the nymph angler's year. What we don't want, unlike all the holidaymakers, is a heatwave, with steady high temperatures and bright sun, when little fish or insect life will move. Far better are warm thundery days, overcast with a ripple. In fact, exactly the sort of weather that sends holidaymakers to the cinema for the afternoon.

Otherwise, it's back to the old formula of early morning and evening sessions. Evenings will see rises to the sedge; in fact the very best of the sedge fishing may come this month – on the evenings that the *caenis* doesn't arrive to hold its spoilsport parties.

Ginger is the colour of July, whether that's in paler shades towards buff and beige, or brighter ones towards amber. Hen pheasant and Carnill ginger dyed materials form the basis of my buzzer, sedge and even olive patterns.

Daphnia peaks now, and some waters look like a giant bowl of pea soup. Now we may have to resort to the less imitative longshank nymphs, with the orange Seal's Fur, longshank bright green Seal's Fur, Invicta Nymph, Booby Nymphs and Palmers, all with their non-specific roles to play.

Almost every nymph is around and busy at this time of the year. Apart from the sedges and *caenis*, though, there only seems to be a smattering of the other insects, never a steady hatch. Buzzers and olives are around, and you'll spoon the odd one or two out of the daphnia cruising fish, but full-blooded hatches seem less common. I'm convinced that a lot of hatches take place at night in July, and that fish then feed quite hard – another reason why they can be difficult to catch during the day.

July is the pleasantest time of the year to be out late and up early. Dawn and dusk repay the lack of sleep by making the senses tingle with anticipation, and showing us a clean time of the day when the world is new, and the tensions of the day are far away. In addition to this spiritual bonus, the fishing can be truly superb. Not a few season-ticket holders on the big waters will make a dawn and dusk pilgrimage, never seeing the daytime holiday crowds, but taking a limit almost every day.

Weed can be an out-and-out problem this month for the bank angler. On the big waters it's time to fish the weedy holes with short casts and lifts, or by suspending a Booby, Damp Dry, or Suspender Buzzer in the holes. On the small waters the weed may seem to be impossible, but it can actually be a bonus. Fish take shelter in the weeds, and even on the brightest day, they can be catchable if you jig a nymph in the gaps in the weed. Sometimes, where there are floating mats of weed, you can actually make a hole yourself with the rod tip, and jiggle the fly in the hole with great success. Having hooked a fish you have to hold on! Usually you net weed and fish together.

The most startling example of this was reported to me from Bridge Farm, the delightful chalk stream series of pools at Old Basing. This is now a brown trout fishery, but in the early days it contained rainbows too. On a little foot-bridge between two pools, just a couple of feet wide, another foot's width of cott had gathered. Anglers cast to the edge of this weed and drew out fish to their flies. But, unbelievably, it was also possible to stand on the little bridge and hook fish literally under your feet. And if you got the first out quickly, there were others prepared to take. All this in water just a couple of feet deep. Somehow the canopy of bridge and weed made the fish feel totally secure.

AUGUST

Everything that's true of July can be true of August. The only slight difference is that the shortening of the days brings the dusk rise back to a more civilised hour. Which is just as well as hot weather this month can make daytime fishing very difficult. The second two weeks of the month can see some cooler weather arrive and fish may feed again during the day; but on the whole this is the month when I wish night fishing was allowed. I'm convinced as I've said, that some very big buzzers come off at night, and this is the month when I'd expect them to show.

Ginger buzzers are high on the menu this month, and while the sedge begin to fade away, the *corixa* start to assume a new importance in the weedbeds. The *caenis* have now gone for good, except for a few sparse hatches early in the month in which it can actually be possible to catch fish on *caenis* imitations.

The *corixa*, through the month, becomes more and more important on the menu. It is odd that the trout only seem to move onto *corixa* when there's little else to eat, but once they do move onto them they feed voraciously. Some of my very best days for numbers of fish have come when *corixa* fishing. Aside from the yellow-bellied adult, there are also what I assume to be immature smaller *corixa* around now. This suggests that July and August are the periods of population explosion that lead, I believe, to the mass dying off of *corixa* that brings extraordinary surface fishing – so look out for that too.

Much of my larger water fishing will be concentrated around the weedbeds this month, for which I may need a boat. But in even the thickest bankside weed there are fishable areas, which very few other anglers are prepared to risk trying. The weedbeds shelter the *corixa*, of course, and also the shoals of newly hatched pinheads. These tiny near-translucent fry are more nymph-sized and shaped (big heads and slim

tails), than fish-shaped, and a silver thorax wound onto a Fraser Nymph
or longshank Cove Nymph can be deadly, on its own, or fished in
conjunction with other nymphs.

Another favourite at this time is the ginger Hackled Pheasant Tail, the
reason being that towards the close of the month there's a return of the
substantial hatches of olives, now in a paler gingery shade.

At the close of the month, as the weather cools, fishing is beginning to
hot up again!

SEPTEMBER

Of all the months in the fishing year this is my favourite, and arguably the
best of the lot. Far from the season fading away, this seems to be boom
time, as everything in the insect world decides to go out with a bang, not
a whimper. The weed begins to go back this month, too. Funnily enough,
the warmer the summer season, the sooner the weed seems to run its life
cycle through and peter out. So we can perhaps get back into some
favourite spots this month, confident in the knowledge that the dying
weedbeds still contain far more food than they did when they began
growing.

The water begins to cool to the optimum temperature again – likely to
be at a healthy level somewhere between the trout's preference for cooler
water, and the insect's for slightly warmer conditions to hatch in. In the
absence of a bright Indian summer (not uncommon in the 70s and 80s),
fish will again feed all day, with the first smell of frost giving a new
urgency to their attempts to put on body weight for the winter or for their
spawning attempts.

There's genuine fat on a grown-on fish in September. Gutting and
cleaning them, you'll find them in superb condition. They also make
excellent eating. Big browns start to move in closer now, and more
specimen fish are caught in this month than any other except April. It's
definitely a time to make time to go fishing.

The olives are back in good numbers this month, paler, gingery, and
smaller than the sizeable spring hatches. *Corixa* too, are still at a peak, and
a smattering of sedges remains. Dark brown and black buzzers return in
numbers.

Outside the scope of this book, big fry come onto the menu. Fish herd them into weedbeds and waterside structures, slamming here and there, taking live fish, then returning to pick up the dead and wounded. Floating fry are one solution, and of course white lures of various types. But some surprising results can be achieved with a big Cove Nymph fished carefully near the fish; or a large Damp Dry pitched into the melée and left.

Daddy-long-legs come onto the menu, and again a longshank Cove can do well, cast near a rising fish; but I also carry some brown Damp Dries with excessively large hackles and cast those out. This is also one time when I've encountered fish feeding on dead shrimps; the static orange Shrimp, or a team of olive and orange Shrimps are well worth trying when no fish show.

Snail migrations occur in this month more than any other. Cork or deerhair bodied flies are the ones to try; in an emergency a longshank orange Seal's Fur will sometimes work. (Ask the fish why!)

Fish will move into quite shallow water this month; both fry and *corixa* draw them in, plus perhaps the beginnings of the spawning urge. Some of these fish will be exceptionally good. It's not a time to fish too light. A minimum of 6 lb nylon should suffice in most conditions – with fish appetites sharpened by the onset of autumn the nylon size may not be a problem.

OCTOBER

Now it's back to the spring spots, the spring methods, and the spring flies. On many large waters fry-feeding takes precedence over everything else, and nymphing can be very disappointing. Early frosts knock back the weeds rapidly, and set the fish off their feed. Midday again becomes the best time to fish, and the deep-grubbed bloodworm, and dark buzzer pupa are your first choice.

The remnants of the year's stocking may be few and far between, and where there is no winter season, new fish may not be coming into the water. It can be hard to find anything that looks like a shoal; and if a fish is caught, this is one time above all others to get quickly back out into the water. It may be a single fish, but it may also be one of a passing shoal of only two or three fish, and you may not have another chance at so many fish all day.

Quite shallow water is still worth a try until the first frosts get hold.

Although the weedbeds will have died down almost out of sight, the fish will still be hunting through the remnants of the only shelter nymphs and fry can find. Avoid all the places that you would avoid in the early season. Dark spawning fish are already moving into those areas – though that said, they will be harder to catch on nymph than lure, and they may not trouble you.

Traditionally, the nymph man's season may be more or less over by mid-October. However, where the water is staying open into the winter, fish still go in, and they still have to eat. How the nymph man can catch them is dealt with in the next section.

NOVEMBER/DECEMBER

These two months of winter fishing mark the end for me of the nymph fisher's actual *fishing* year. Much of the fishing will be with lures for newly stocked fish. There's little food about to teach these fish to adapt to normal feeding habits – unlike their spring-stocked counterparts. As for the surviving fish, from in-season stockings, they'll be well blitzed and depleted by now. But, like a struggling and defeated army, they'll know all about scratching a living out from what food is available. Their menu will consist of caddis, bloodworm, shrimp, snails, leeches, and quite a bit of fry, though these small fish will be gradually retreating offshore into deeper water.

The fish will once again lie deep, but both the spawning urge, and the occasional warmer day will see them moving into shallower water. Some clean fish will even hang around what may be warmer water coming in from land drains, creeks, and springs, and the nymph can sort them out from the more aggressive black fish.

As the weather gets more severe the fish will fall back to what is often warmer deeper water. They'll be more sluggish, disinclined to go racing after a fly, and a nymph fisherman's slow and steady approach will score whatever you choose to tie on the end. Dark Booby Nymphs – claret, black and red – will now be first choices. With less weed the Boobies will be fishable on a shorter leader, slow and deep. A Zulu Nymph on a sink tip, or a black Tadpole, will also score, trundled along slow and deep. Small dark wet flies will often be an improvement on standard lures.

On warmer days, look for brief midday rises to small dark buzzers.

133

These are more common on the small waters which, as ever, warm up more quickly. Short dressed Spiders seem especially effective at this time.

The weed has virtually all gone, the Christmas carols are playing in the shops, and our thoughts turn sensibly to hearth and home. Call me a traditionalist, but I really would miss some sort of close season each year. And, as it is, the weather seems determined to back up my case, by making the other two months of the year too unpleasant to make me want to fish at all.

JANUARY/FEBRUARY

The great thing about nymph fishing is that you don't actually have to leave the house to enjoy the sport – the actual fishing calls for so much background work. First there are the flies to be dressed. I really can't imagine that you could fish the nymph for long without taking up flydressing, as using the spoon, and matching the contents is such an integral part of the sport. At the same time there are entomological books to be read, and hopefully instructional ones like this one. And talking of books, there's a great need for every angler to keep a diary, especially the nymph man who follows the procession of the seasons and insect hatches with more interest than most.

This is also the time for tackle maintenance. Modern rods need little work, but it is worth oiling the reel seat and wiping down the rod with soapy water. Modern ceramic rings of the Fuji and Seymo types need little maintenance, but it is very worthwhile checking rod rings, as even a tiny crack or flaw can ruin a fly line when it's stripped or cast through the rings. A plasticiser properly applied to the fly line when it's stored will do away with the problem of tight coils in the line and delay the inevitable cracking; a moth repellant does little harm popped into the flyboxes.

One use of diaries is to help you make a shortlist of the top dozen patterns that you wouldn't want to be without. Now's the time to dress up half a dozen of each. As the season progresses you'll tie up others to add to these. And when one of your 'specials' works, it's one of the best moments in the sport.

One last thing for the winter, which can be fascinating, is to set up a tank to watch the various aquatic insects and bugs close up. Like me, you'll discover that so voracious are *corixa* that they'll actually chew their way through a lump of meat. You'll be able to watch the swimming and movements of the various creatures, and how they make their hatches.

Of course, in the controlled environment of your own home, it's always summer, so don't be surprised if you come home one day, as I did, to find a room full of sedges! On another occasion I carefully peeled a caddis from its case. Rapidly it set about building a new one from whatever was available. In this case that was some aquarium grit that I'd crumbled up, and soon it was proudly sporting a bright blue case!

I can't stress too highly the importance of observation to the nymph angler. Just as the expected features listed in this calendar come along, so do the unexpected: I've even heard of sedges hatching in mid-winter. So it can't be stressed too much that you should never go fishing with a preconceived idea of what will happen. You've always got to sum up all the clues on the day, and put together your tactics to match.

You also need imagination, to think what might be happening below the surface. This to me is so often the difference between the successful angler, and the average man: both have access to all the information – but the expert has the imagination and vision to apply it successfully.

135

15 · WHERE NEXT? – SOME THOUGHTS ON THE FUTURE OF NYMPHING

The new generation of trout anglers have seen a lot of changes over the last 20 years, and though the pace of change seems to be slowing, it would be madness to suggest that the sport won't go on developing for as long as we're able to fish for trout – which may or may not be a pity.

One word of warning: there are few things that are new in the sport. You've only got to come up with something that's new to you, and 20 people will claim it as their own. I know, because it's happened to me on so many occasions. When in this book, and in my catalogue, I use the word new, I mean what is new to me.

One interesting development that seems to be genuinely new, and may change the way we make up our leaders, is the introduction of braided butt pieces. At the time of writing I haven't tried them, but anglers who have are quite impressed. But as soon as they're in common use, endless letters will hit the magazine pages, all claiming that the writer's grandfather used to braid his own cat gut (or even horse hair) leaders a hundred years ago. No doubt he did, and no doubt they worked!

NYMPHS ON THE LEAD LINE

As you may recall from the buzzer chapter of this book, I'm convinced that there are some very large nymphs hatching from great depth in some of our reservoirs. I didn't fish nymphs on the lead line when the method boomed at Rutland Water, but those that worked varying quantities of lead-cored line in the depths caught some very fine browns. Gutted, or spooned, these often contained large buzzers, along with leeches, and hog lice.

Some anglers even fished nymphs deep on the easy days, and took some fish. But no one has really worked at this method. Big fish, especially browns, do live deep, and can be elusive. A deep-fished nymph may be a solution – but by deep I mean 25 feet and deeper. The only really efficient way to fish these depths is by wind-trailing a lead-cored line in the classic Rutland style. Big fish on the take experience not only the pull of the boat, but the heavy inertia of a moving lead line. However big the nymphs may be at that depth, anything bigger than a size 8 hook will be totally unnatural. Small hooks will often straighten when faced with that kind of pull.

I've found some very short-shanked, but heavy-wired hooks, with which I dress some small salmon flies. But a lifelike buzzer can also be tied on these hooks, and some early experiments suggest that they'll hook fish at considerable depths.

Leadlining has come in for a lot of stick from anglers who thought that their way was the only one, be it nymph or traditional drifting. But many of those with the loudest voices had never tried it, or tried and failed. Certainly to suggest that the method lacks skill is totally wrong. In truth, to fish a leadline properly requires a great deal of skill. When fishing a floater, we can work out roughly what depth our flies are fishing at, but how do you know when your flies are just off the bottom in 40 feet of water? Or how do you consistently cover fish that are 10 feet off the bottom, in 40 feet of water? You must account for the length of the line out, its density, and the speed of the drifting boat.

I feel that deep nymph fishing is virtually the only method left to be properly explored, and the techniques necessary will bear little resemblance to the more accepted forms of nymphing. The obvious way to start is by trailing a nymph or nymphs behind a slowly drifting boat. But do check the fishery rules first as trailed lines are illegal on some waters. Yet, sadly, it seems that the deep water boom time of the early 80s is over at Rutland. Perhaps a new giant reservoir will arise, and I'll have the chance of taking these experiments further.

Just to prove that it can work, I should recall a day when there was the impetus to try the deep nymph, and it produced some excellent results.

Boat fishing on Rutland one August day in 1982, the top-of-the-water sport was really poor. Down the South Arm shallows, my boat partner and I had tried every method and presentation of a nymph you care to think of – all without success, barring one fish on a Sedge Pupa, and a missed take and a fish on a Hare's Ear. Reluctantly we decided to shift up the arm to deeper water in search of some other fish.

Anglers who know Rutland will be aware that coming back into the 'main pool' in front of the dam, often means that stockies or the odd big brown are the only fish you're likely to contact. Back in 1982, there was still some excellent deep water fishing to be had along the edges of that area, not least on the drift between the 'Fantasy Island' corner of the dam, down past the Three Trees and the church towards the Yacht Club.

In August there are quite a few fish to be had around the 'boils' at Rutland. These bubbling sources of oxygen attract and hold good numbers of stockies, and occasionally some better fish. We headed that way, but we never got there, as we spotted a boat setting up for another drift along the Yacht Club Bay, and as I thought I recognised one of the occupants, we set off in that direction.

I was right, it was that master lead line angler Fred Wagstaffe. In reply to my careful approach and shouted questions Fred generously told us that they'd done quite well, taking between the pair of them in his boat, 10 fish, 8 browns among them. He'd been on the rudder all day, with a lead line, and a large white Waggy, his controversial lure with a plastic sand eel tail, producing a seductive wiggle. He advised us to try the same, and stop 'messing around on top'. (Fred's record with deep caught fish entitles him to talk like that!)

Moving on up the bank we had a chat. Neither of us were keen on the lead. We didn't have one with us, either. I did have a full lead-preg weight-forward 8 for my Booby fishing. My partner, confirmed top water man that he was, didn't even have a sinking line. But, he said, if I wanted to experiment, he'd fish out the front of the boat. So we set up the boat with a pair of drogues to slow it down. For convenience we would have to fish broadside on – a broadside boat drifts a lot faster than one point or stern down – so we used the drogues that each of us had brought, one on each corner of the boat.

I set up the powerful 10 foot rod, and put a 20 foot leader on with a dropper 6 feet up. My point fly was intended to be sacrificial. It would, if I got the line deep enough, perhaps bounce the bottom. But the dropper would fish clear, I hoped. Remembering the hog lice, I put a Leaded Hare's Ear longshank size 8 on the point – larger than a hog louse but a passable copy and the lead would help to get everything down. After a lengthy sort through the box, I did what I always do when in doubt about the dropper, and opted for a size 12 Black Spider.

I was able to push a few yards of line against the breeze out of the back of the boat, and I followed the cast by feeding out a long line, feeling for tell-tale bumps. Some 60 or 70 yards of backing went out, when I felt a bump, and, deciding it was the bottom, I began a slow retrieve. The line felt very heavy, as it would so far behind the boat.

My retrieve was to pull back about 20 yards of line, in figure-of-eight, then let it slip back in pauses, holding the line and feeling for takes. Casting was unnecessary.

About opposite Normanton Church, I had a heavy pull that contrasted with the gentle bumps of the point fly as it touched bottom. I started to pull in line, but after a few seconds' solid resistance, the fish was gone. Fortunately I followed my usual practice after losing a fish, of checking the flies. The size 12 Spider was completely opened out. Obviously all that drag was too much for a small hook at that depth.

That sent me grubbing through the box again, until I came up with some freak size 8 Buzzers that I had virtually discarded as too big for practical use. One of those went on the dropper, and to my delight after only 10 minutes of drift, everything went solid again, the line actually slipping through my fingers, and this one didn't come off. After a superb battle, a brown of 3 lb 10 oz came to the net.

Spooned, the fish had a bellyful of louse, and the odd few large dark brown buzzer pupae. I had little choice, though, but to stay with the black Buzzer I had on. And at that depth there would have been little light for the fish to have made clever comparisons of colour.

By around 8 pm I'd taken three nice browns, another at 2 lb 12 oz, and a superb hen fish of around 5 lb which alone of the three, took the point Hare's Ear. Fishing in front of the boat, and unsurprisingly over such deep water, my partner had taken nothing. But now a sprinkle of buzzers started to hatch and the odd fish showed.

Always a lover of floating line tactics, I soon switched when my partner started catching fish on a Fraser Nymph. He took a limit by the close, and I had seven fish. But without the deepwater tactics, I certainly wouldn't have caught anything exceptional.

Roll on the days when this is possible again – though I have a nasty feeling that whoever is running the Water Authorities a few years hence, may have financial restraints which will stop them ever considering a stocking and fishery programme like the mighty one that made Rutland such a special water for a few sweet years.

WILD WATER NYMPHING

Another ambition, and something I may well see in my lifetime, is to prove that the nymph will regularly catch good wild browns in the waters where only traditional flies seem to score. These waters are mainly in Scotland and Ireland, where traditionalism still seems to rule. But many of those loch and lough browns must take nymphs regularly, to survive, and I can't believe that the short-line bank, and drifting boat tactics, are the only way to catch them.

I know that some fishing has been done with nymphs in Ireland, and that fish have been taken from the static boat. But my ears still prick up with interest when I'm told of the expert Irish boatman who could point out an area where he said the fish fed deep on shrimp and snail, yet he'd never fished nymph style at anchor there.

WINTER FISHING

Now that there's no close season for rainbows, we're going to find more and more opportunities to experiment with nymphing in the winter. A surprising number of insects do continue to put in an appearance during the winter, especially small dark buzzers and related species, while bloodworm, cased caddis, *corixa*, shrimps and leeches are present all year round. Severe weather may wash other nymphs out of their hides, and one angling friend has had considerable success with an earthworm pattern on a tandem hook mount in flooded waters.

One thing is already clear: floating lines, slow sinkers, and nymph style retrieves seem to produce the better fish when they're over comparatively shallow water (which they often are, the unsuccessful spawning urge being strong in even the clean rainbows, and shallow water often being warmer). In more severe weather, when trout may sulk in deep water, the Booby series comes into its own, and grubbing the flies along deep has provided some spectacular sport, especially down at Datchet, the huge concrete bowl in west London.

NIGHT FISHING

Most experts agree that very large brown trout come in closest, and swim nearest to the top, at night. Of course, the very nature of poaching problems makes it unlikely that the owners would allow night fishing – but what an opportunity if they did. Imagine the sharpening of the nymphing skills, fishing the darkest night, sea trout style, by touch, with a large longshank BP on the point, and a waking Palmer or Booby on the dropper. Imagine trickling the fly around with only the sensitive pads of your fingertips between you and the take. Imagine the concentration involved, and the huge improvement in your skills when you get back in the daylight.

There are few wild loughs and lochs where you can try this. Speaking for myself, a chance can't come soon enough. But what a pity the English waters can't trust their anglers enough to let them try the night sport. There's no question that they'd pick up the otherwise often 'wasted' brown trout.

CATCH-AND-RELEASE

I certainly feel that the future of trout fishing may lie more and more with catch-and-release trout fisheries. With a steady increase in stocking costs, it seems simply that the price of a reasonable day's trout fishing can no longer be kept at an affordable level. Take Rutland Water: I can't help feeling that the high pricing policy in 1984 and 85 came close to ruining what could and should be Europe's best trout fishery. The average angler could no longer afford to keep paying the price week-by-week.

As I write this, I feel that a solution might be a two fish limit, after which the angler would be able to release fish. A day's sport could then be realistically priced, and anglers could fish without a trace of the

Dawn at Rutland Water. Starting in the pre-dawn hour is the closest most nymph fishermen get to night fishing. Yet big browns were moving close in when the picture was taken.

fishmongering frame of mind that suggests it's important to take a good bag to 'pay' for the price of the ticket.

A coarse angler would certainly consider a 20 lb carp far too valuable to kill it – although on the other hand that fish can successfully spawn, which a rainbow cannot. Yet with modern hybrids, triploids, and all-female rainbows, there's no reason why even rainbow stockies shouldn't last through several seasons. And a brown trout may live 15 years or more, so even a 6 lb brown could be regarded as an investment in the future if carefully returned.

Nowadays I return far more trout than I kill – a couple for spooning and the pot, and any others back, hopefully a little wiser.

142

Returning a 4lb brown trout with many years growth left in it. At many waters such fish will successfully spawn in feeder streams. At the Eye Brook, Pitsford Water, Tittesworth, and Ladybower wild fish are common.

NEW MATERIALS

Like most nymph anglers, I thought that I'd never stray from natural materials when dressing my favourite patterns. But I was wrong. Restrictions on our materials seem to be mounting. For years my nymphs relied mainly on wool and seal's fur, with the odd bit of pheasant tail. Now even this seems threatened; soon seal's fur may be unavailable. But things have changed for me. I now sell, and use often, very good synthetic seal's fur; the red seal's fur Bloodworm I have used for years now has a plastic body. The old nylon rib on the buzzers has given way to polypropylene; blended fur threatens to oust the old woollen patterns. Carefully dyed mole has made my old thorax materials redundant.

There's no reason to suppose that other new materials won't catch my eye, and further transform my patterns. And if I were you, I'd experiment with anything that takes your fancy.

Of course as I warned at the start of this chapter, not all that's new in fishing, is actually new. Take my blended fur: you can trace mixed fur dubbings back through the great Northampton angler, Cyril Inwood, through the works of Kingsmill Moore, to the original Tup's nymph dressing, and no doubt, far beyond.

But we each evolve differently as anglers, which is one of the things that makes the sport so much fun. New discoveries mean that every trip can be a voyage of exploration. Hopefully you'll try many of the methods in this book, and find that they work for you. When they do, they'll give you as much pleasure of discovery as they did for me, in the first place, and all the other anglers from whom I've learnt so much.

16 · THE BIRTH OF THE FRASER NYMPH AND OTHER STORIES

I like to think that all the best nymphing patterns are the result of deep thought and observation. Take the Cove Nymph – its universal success was probably far from Arthur Cove's mind when he tied the pattern to match some large chestnut Grafham buzzers. But the fly has gone on to be deadly on waters where large buzzers are rarely seen, catching fish that are eating everything *but* buzzers.

A similar process produced my best-ever pattern, the Fraser Nymph. It was back in 1976 in the drought, and I was giving Grafham a great deal of my attention. In the Gaynes Cove area, large fawnish buzzers were appearing on a lot of afternoons, and though I was catching the odd fish here and there, I felt that my results weren't matching up to my opportunities. Scratching my head for a better imitation of the buzzers, I suddenly happened upon hen pheasant, which matched the colour perfectly. I settled down at the vice and tied my original nymphs on a size 14 longshank.

Back on a bright blustery day at Gaynes Cove, I went around to the north bank of the cove, and with the wind behind me, I waded through the soft mud to cast across and down the wind. I had a size 10 Brown Buzzer on the dropper, 8 feet above a Fraser Nymph on the point.

I had to cast over my left shoulder, and got out the longest line possible. After about two minutes of the flies sinking and drifting, I started a very slow figure-of-eight retrieve. On my fifth cast there was a gentle pluck, which I took for weed, and I lifted the rod to flick it free. As I did so, everything went tight, and my line sliced through the water. It took a while to get on top, but when I did, I was delighted to land a super hen rainbow of 4 ½ lb. I was more than a little staggered to get such a beautiful fish, but when I spooned it, it had a dozen or more fawn buzzers, and a couple of bloodworm in it. With even more confidence I waded back and was delighted to take a 2 ½ lb rainbow after a couple more casts.

Still not totally convinced that a new fly could have such a dramatic effect so quickly, I swapped the flies over and with the Fraser on the dropper, it took all of 20 minutes before I got another trout. This was another beauty of 2 lb, so with three nice fish to my credit, it was time to experiment and I spent an hour and a half trying every other fly in the box. A sharp snatch snapped a Black Buzzer off the point, but apart from that, not a tickle. So back went the Fraser on the point. By now I was convinced that the fish had moved on.

Not expecting a pull I missed the first one, but went on to take a 24 lb 8 oz limit. It was a most remarkable first test for the fly. The Fraser Nymph continued to score at Gaynes Cove, but since that day, it has become my standby pattern once the weather has warmed up.

The original fly didn't have the legs of the present pattern, but, unlike other buzzer patterns, it wasn't taken around the hook bend. Instead it had tails. While tails have never been discarded, they don't always seem to make much difference, and well-chewed tailless flies still catch.

Funnily enough, despite originating the fly, I soon suffered the fate of many other fly 'inventors'. A customer asked me for some Fraser Nymphs, but rejected mine. The proper pattern he said, had a silver rib. I actually had to show him my picture in a magazine before he'd agree that mine was the true pattern. As you'll see in Chapter 17, the Fraser Nymph has a fawn cotton rib. I found that changing it for a green cotton rib, and adding an olive mole thorax, gave the whole fly an attractive olive tinge, and increased its success in an olive hatch. But the original still catches fish under all sorts of conditions, and if it remains my only lasting claim to fame, I'll be well pleased with it.

FISHING IN THE CLOUDS

As I've said previously, I fished at Grafham a lot in 1976. The reason was my huge good fortune in capturing a 7 lb 6 oz rainbow the season before, which won me a season ticket at the water.

On this particular day, I whizzed down the A1 in time for an afternoon session. It was a lovely June day for sunbathing, not fishing, with a gentle breeze and only the odd cloud drifting over a clear blue sky. I fished on the north shore, making my way round to the bay that had seen the capture of my big rainbow. The bay has a pylon on its point, and is the next one up from Church Farm.

There was just one angler on the point opposite the pylon, and as I passed I asked him how the fishing was. With his wife sunbathing on the bank behind him, he was sure that it was too bright – at any rate he wasn't catching, and he'd been there since 9 am.

I went where there was a gentle ripple in the bay, rather than out on the point with a back wind. My tackle was a floating line, a long leader rubbed down with mud, with a Pheasant Tail Nymph on the point and a Black Spider on the dropper. In this position I had to cast (right-handed) over my left shoulder – a very useful skill on occasions – and for about half an hour I did my usual thing of mixing up speeds and depths of retrieve, without success.

I was about to have a break, and a think, when I noticed the sky clouding over. One big fluffy cloud was obscuring the sun. Halfway through the next retrieve came a gentle pluck which I missed through surprise. Next cast my first couple of yards of line came back, then stopped, and with a steady draw away, I lifted the rod and was into a rainbow of 1½ lb. It had taken the 12 longshank Pheasant Tail.

The spoon revealed a little bit of everything – the odd buzzer pupa and larva, a few caddis, one or two shrimps and some daphnia. This is usually a good sign: fish feeding non-specifically can be easy to catch. But as the buzzers were green, I swapped the Spider for a lime green Buzzer, size 12. The point fly would make an adequate imitation of a caddis. Wading back out, I had a nice fish on the second cast. It had taken the Lime Buzzer.

This success brought the chap from the point to see what was happening. I told him how I'd caught the fish, and suggested he move round and join me in the patch of ripple. He didn't fancy the left shoulder casting position, though, and stayed where he was. I waded back out, and fished on for around an hour and a half without success. The sun was back out, and none of the few little fluffy clouds had blocked it off.

147

Once again I was on my way out for a rest when I realised that another cloud was coming over the sun. I stayed in the water waiting for it. A good long chuck across the ripple, and I let everything settle, starting the retrieve just as the cloud covered the sun. Halfway through a steady retrieve, the line stopped and I tightened into what seemed a much better fish. After a five minute tussle I beached a rainbow of around 4 lb.

By the time the fish was landed the little cloud had passed on. I waded out in bright sunshine again, and fished fruitlessly for half an hour. By now I'd cottoned on – the fish only fed in the cloud cover, when they either rose up in the water, or ran in from deeper water. Possibly, too, any flash from my nylon was less obvious in cloud cover.

I moved in and out of the water, resting on the bank during bright spells, wading in to fish the cloud cover for five or ten minutes. With these brief interludes I managed six fish by around 7 pm, all but the first on Lime Buzzers. By the time the sun started to slip from the sky, a cold east wind had sprung up and though the light was perfect, sport was over for the day.

LET THEM HANG THEMSELVES

Corixa time at Eye Brook is not to be missed. In late August a few years back when I planned to spend the afternoon there, there was only one place to fish: in the Stoke Dry weedbeds. The wind was north east, with plenty of cloud cover.

About 300 yards to the right of the road, the weedbeds push out some 25 feet from the bank and it's possible to wade out almost to the edge of the weed. By mid-summer the water here is pretty shallow, some 2 to 4 feet. When trout are hard on *corixa* they often show as they work the edge of the weedbeds. On this day, I saw enough fish to make me quietly confident.

A floating line was combined with a 15 foot leader of 4 lb nylon, well rubbed down with mud, and with one of my standard yellow Corixas on the point. Keeping a camouflage screen of weed – about 6 feet – in front of me, I began to work out short casts. Straightaway, I was covering fish, but they seemed reluctant to take. Perhaps I was fishing below them. Out came the grease pot, and I greased the leader to within 12 inches of the fly. That brought immediate response from the trout.

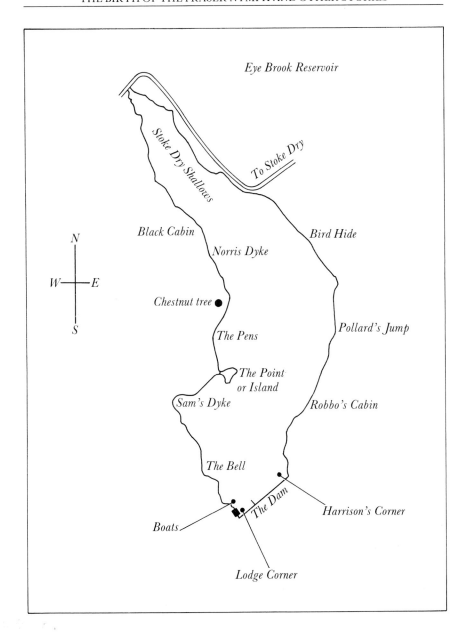

Fig 22

The spots Gordon mentions are shown on this map of his favourite water

The problem now was that I couldn't hook the takes. Both steady draws and a figure-of-eight produced bumps and bangs, but the fish just wouldn't stay on the hook. The obvious thing to do was to check the hook. Sometimes a stone, a bit of weed, a low backcast, or a bony trout mouth, can turn over the point of the hook. But this hook was perfect. Obviously I had my presentation right – I was getting a knock virtually every cast. I tried a continuous very fast figure-of-eight, and eventually this produced two fish. But as often happens at the Eye Brook, the fish called it a day around 6 pm, stopped showing, and I didn't have another offer.

That day must have been one of the most frustrating few hour's fishing I've ever experienced. We all have blank days when the fish aren't interested, and we take it in our stride. But when the fish are tugging and pulling all day . . .

That evening I searched my mind for a solution. I even dreamt trout that night. I came up with a theory: I was fishing such a short line that when the fish came up behind the fly, and tried to turn away, the short tight line pulled the fly out of their mouths.

On the next day I had such a bad dose of trout fever that I needed a day off work to recover. The weather was identical to the day before, and I headed for the same spot. The trout were still there and still showing. I started to fish in the same manner as the day before: I got frustrating pulls and tugs.

It was time to test the theory. I had decided that I had to give these fish enough rope to hang themselves. They needed enough line to swim up to the fly, take it, turn down, and swim away – when they should be hooked in the scissors. On the next cast, I held the rod up higher, allowing the line to form a swingtip for me, and watched that for takes. A take made the line draw away, and the fish felt the minimum resistance. It worked dramatically. I lost count of the trout I hooked that afternoon; I kept just six, and returned more than fifty more, both browns and rainbows.

I'd learnt a lot. It won't always work, but this is yet another useful technique when fish are apparently 'taking short'. It can even happen with a lure. When it does, get that rod up, and let them hang themselves!

WHEN THE LURE WON

'Right,' I told Steve Windsor, 'let's get down to the Brook, and I'll show you some real nymphing.' My confidence was based on my personal success in the past few days, and the fact that a couple of my customers had reported that the fish were exactly where I'd have expected, in the conditions.

On the way down to what I thought would be the 'hot spot' area, we fished over various other good spots, trying all my best early-season nymphing patterns and tactics: no joy. We eventually reached the 'hot spot' area among the willows to the left at the bottom of Stoke Dry road. The wind was blowing straight into the bays here.

We fished a variety of nymphing methods without success, until Steve picked up his luring rod, with a tiny size 12 black and green Tadpole on the end. This rapidly brought him several fish, mostly browns. The fish were hard in against the shore in barely 2 feet of water among some dead weeds. We took the boat in closer and closer, until Steve was picking up fish regularly.

I tried every nymph in the book. The floating line or sink-tip and slow retrieve always seemed to result in weed on the flies. Steve, on the other hand, was fishing a fast-sinker and literally chopping his way through the dead scraps of marginal weed. The routine was to ignore the first few taps – which were always weed – then concentrate for the takes which almost always followed as the fly left the weed.

After half a dozen or so fish, we moved a little along the bank to the right of the road. Down here, the thick summer ranunculus weed was just a memory of dead stems on the bottom. In addition an oozing brown slick of silt flowed along the edge, whipped up by the strong wind.

It took a while to find the fish here, but once located they were right on the edge of this 3 or 4 yard wide marginal slick. Once again it was chop, chop, through the weed, then a firm take.

I'd joined Steve on the lure now, but every now and again I'd take up the nymph rod – but, though I must have been fishing through the same fish, not a touch did I get.

We ended that day with more than a dozen fish each, but not one took a nymph. On reflection, my best chance of fishing imitatively that day would have been a Booby Nymph trickled through the same area – but when fish are coming every other cast, it takes a brave man to change his tactics!

STEAL A RISE WITH A SINK-TIP

When I used to work for British Steel, I was able, like a lot of other shift workers, to grab an odd morning or afternoon by the water almost at will. One early shift in June I was due to finish at 2 pm, and all morning I'd kept an eye on the weather, sometimes popping out of the foundry to see what the wind was like.

The conclusions of my weather watching were not encouraging. It was a bright cloudless day, perfect for sunbathing, but dreadful for fishing. I kept thinking what a struggle the boats on the Eye Brook would be having; the only chance of some real sport would come towards the evening. Now the Eye Brook can be a pig of a fishery in the evenings, and unlike most other waters, sport there often switches off around 6 pm. But I decided to try an evening session regardless, so after a shower and a meal, I drove back to the Brook, and around 4.15 pm I was coming down past Stoke Dry village with its haunted church.

I always approach the water from this direction as it gives me an excellent chance to drive around the water and try to sum things up. On this occasion the wind was from the south, and was predictably nice and warm. On this wind I like to anchor off the Island, a classic spot where the fish run onto the submerged finger going out from the Island – in water between 4 and 10 feet – out of the deeps, and you can often intercept them by swinging a nymph around on the southerly wind.

Imagine my disappointment at seeing two boats already in position as I drove past the Pens. And no sign of any occupants either, so they were obviously sunbathing the day away in the bottom of the boats. From that I could conclude that there wasn't much happening with the fishing. Never mind – they might move on. I took out my boat ticket at the lodge, signed the book, and paused for a chat with two anglers who were seeking some shade from the sun in the lodge. Since 8.30 am, they had managed just one trout on a trolled Baby Doll. (There was a little lesson to remember here as well – one of the anglers had had his shirt off all day, and looked like a well-boiled lobster. Sunburn is much more likely in a boat than on the land – there's no shade, and the sun bounces back off the water. So it's wise to wear a long sleeved shirt, preferably one you can dip in the water and put back on in severe heat!)

After a while, I decided it was time to get out on the water. My usual comment on these occasions is that I won't catch fish sitting in the lodge.

'You won't catch one out there either,' one of the pair replied.

I set up two rods, one with a floater, and 18 foot leader to 4 lb, and a green Buzzer and olive Buzzer, both size 14. A sink-tip was set up with a 6 lb point and the same leader, with a size 12 Red Larva on the point, for grubbing deep, and an olive Buzzer on the dropper.

I made my way down towards the Island or Point. It's not quite an Island for most of the year, but only a few feet of dry land separate it from the main bank. I took an echo sounder over this area once, and it was clear just how attractive the two sunken points of the Island would be to trout, sheltering in deep water nearby, then running onto these shallows to feed.

Unfortunately the boats were still there, though no one was fishing in them: it was time to think again. I rowed past the two boats, hoping they'd soon move, and anchored over 15 feet of water at the mouth of the Pens, the weedy little bay to the north side of the Island.

It occurred to me that this wasn't a bad idea anyway. Here was some deeper water in a very 'fishy' area, and in these light conditions fish weren't going to come up for a fly, or onto the shallows. One bonus was a rolling, round topped wave coming steadily down the reservoir. It seemed hard to believe that, apart from the sun, fish wouldn't take in such otherwise perfect conditions.

But there was one thing missing: not a sign of a hatch anywhere, not even a gently drifting empty shuck. This is a typical Eye Brook situation on a bright day. There's nothing hatching, and although we know there are fish to be caught down deep, they simply won't take. Then the next day, in identical conditions, they will. Trout don't feed all the time, just like humans, when the larder is as well stocked as it is on most June reservoirs. And as we've seen, a lot of feeding may happen at night in high summer.

Another boat drifted by, and recognising my disreputable hat they came over to ask how I was doing. Of course, I hadn't started. Their results were two trout on a Whisky fly – trolled again.

I started to fish slowly round in front of the boat, searching the water with my deep nymph, By 7 pm I hadn't had a touch. Once again, I wound in and took a break enjoying the summer evening on a reservoir I always find beautiful. After about 20 minutes I started again, and a few casts later, I had a take. I was so surprised I nearly missed it, but my late

153

reaction still hooked what proved to be a brown of a pound and a bit. In went the spoon, and apart from two still lively buzzers, the fish was empty. Clearly it had just started to feed, after fasting and lying doggo all day.

A few minutes later another fish was hooked. This brown took the Bloodworm pattern, and as if to prove my theory mathematically, this one had a dozen green and olive pupae, many still alive, in its stomach. At last they were feeding.

By 8 pm I had four nice browns in the boat, and throughout this successful period I'd not seen a fly, or a rise on the surface. But though the feeding session had started down deep, I now started to get takes on the drop. I hooked a couple, and this time the spoon showed some pupae of a silvery appearance, their shucks just beginning to inflate with pumped-in gas. The odd buzzer, inevitably, started to appear on the surface and in the air.

Now with the light fading (it was approaching 9 pm) and the wind dropping, takes were suddenly few and far between. There was the odd tap on the drop, and though no fish were showing on top, I was obviously fishing underneath them. Time for the floater.

Ten minutes with that line produced my first fish, and a stirring in one of the nearby boats. A cry of what's happening soon followed, and I explained that a few olive buzzers were hatching and I'd had seven fish. As they hurried into action, I didn't have the heart to tell them that they'd missed a couple of hours of interesting sport.

I finished that evening with ten fish, which proved to be the best on the water that night. Most anglers had had two to four fish, however, and nearly all of them had come after 9 pm. Of course, if I hadn't had my sink-tip to fall back on, I would have been in the same boat. But this time it let me steal a rise on the others.

FUN AT THE FISH PONDS

This is a story with several lessons. One is never to assume that fish will behave the way you'd like them to, despite the current feeding trend. Another is that some small areas of a large water can have a hatch all to themselves – and a resident shoal of fish too. Yet another is that fish, like humans, really appreciate a change of diet from time to time, even in the middle of a comparatively settled feeding pattern. Sometimes even a fry feeding fish will take a few nymphs as an hors d'oeuvre, or as dessert. The final lesson is always to rinse your washing carefully!

Steve Cole rang me one day, while I was particularly busy at the vice. Steve was at the time the advertisement manager for *Trout Fisherman*, and in the course of discussing business with me, he asked if I'd been fishing recently. I hadn't, through pressure of work, but I had heard that some super fish were being caught down the Rutland North Arm on big white lures, sidecast. Not perhaps my favourite method, but when fish are feeding on fry, I'm happy to imitate that item on the trout's menu too.

Steve's enthusiasm as a relative newcomer to the sport was fired by this information and he rapidly persuaded me to take an afternoon off and give these fish a try. A couple of days later we were tackling up in the Rutland car park, with powerful rods, lead-preg lines, and size four white Muddlers. Not quite the style of this book I'll admit, but effective.

It was an overcast June day, with rather a cool south east wind, and the odd light shower. We expected plenty of fish on the top, and after motoring down the North Arm, I was a bit staggered not to see at least one fish showing.

We tried a run on the rudder from the Barnsdale Woods, and past the mouth of Dickinson's Bay without any results. A change to a pair of smaller Tadpoles brought me a 1 ½ lb brown, as bright as a fresh run sea trout, and full of daphnia. He certainly wasn't one of the fry feeders we'd heard about. By this time Steve was more trailing the line than casting, and a heavy shower did nothing to cheer him up.

I turned to Steve to console him, and nearly fell out of the boat laughing. In the heavy rain, foam was oozing from every pore of his showerproof jacket. I soon discovered it had been recently washed and obviously not rinsed too well. The casting and retrieving had left Steve with foaming armpits.

Steve really deserved a break after all my promises, and with the fish simply not interested out in the main arm, I saw a few swifts moving down at the mouth of the old Burleigh Fish Ponds. I set up the boat to run in there, and as we drifted in I spotted the odd olive on the surface. I had the Muddler on again, and as we were halfway across the ponds, a quick short cast at the treelined shore produced amazing results. The fly hit the top, there was a swirl and it disappeared.

155

After a superb battle Steve netted a 4½ lb rainbow for me. This was more like it, and as the area was so small and repeated drifting would put down fish, I suggested anchoring. Very slowly we motored out again, and anchored in the mouth.

I used to fish these ponds for carp long before I started trouting, and before Rutland was ever dreamt of. At the entrance to the ponds there was a dam wall which was bulldozed away before the area was flooded. There's a gulley in this area which was gouged out by the water coming through the dam and meandering up to where the tower now stands. Either side though, there's just 6 feet or so of water. Fish tend to hang in the gulley in up to 20 feet of water, coming out occasionally to feed.

Anchored up, we paused to spoon the trout, fully expecting to find large roach or perch fry in it. To our amazement it had olive nymphs, and a few large brown buzzer pupae in it. That certainly wasn't one of the fry feeders either. Obviously I would be smart to try a floater and nymphs. Steve persevered with his sinker and a Baby Doll he'd tied himself.

I'd almost finished setting up my tackle, when Steve hooked a very good fish. The reel literally screamed (a rarer thing than you'd think, reading some writers), and 50 yards of line followed the fish in one long run. Steve got it under control after several minutes, and got it back to the boat. The next fireworks came when the fish got near the side, dived under the boat, and Steve was holding a rod so hooped that the tip was almost under the water.

Steve obviously ties a good knot, for that fish took more punishment than I've ever seen used. Eventually after several more heart-stopping moments I netted a superb hen rainbow of about 5½ lb for Steve. He just sat trembling while I dispatched it, and took the Baby Doll out of the scissors.

With Steve's previous experience of small waters, he'd never encountered anything like that fish. Indeed it was unquestionably the fish of a lifetime for anyone. Mind you, he is an angler whose first ever rainbow weighed 3 lb!

Of course, there was no way I could persuade him to try a nymph now, and he persevered with the Baby Doll, while I began to fish with the nymph. There were quite simply some superb fish in the small area in front of the boat. I could, on cool reflection, see the odd swirl and flattening of the waves that spelled feeding fish, and with a lot of

156

confidence now, I cast across the wind and let the flies swing round. On the first cast, halfway through the first retrieve, the line stopped and went solid. The resulting 3 lb brown was full of olive nymphs and brown buzzers, some still alive. We'd obviously arrived as the fish came on the feed.

Steve's big fish had much the same in it, bar a couple of roach fry which convinced Steve to stay with the Baby Doll.

I got five exceptional fish on the Fraser Nymph that day, the smallest from the Fish Ponds being 2 lb 10 oz. Out in the main reservoir, nothing was hatching and few fish were caught. But here in the Fish Ponds, the land had been under water for at least 50 years, and a well-established population of nymphs had held these feeding fish in place.

THE MOST DIFFICULT FISH

Someone once said that you reach a stage in fishing, after wanting to catch the most fish, then the biggest, when you want to catch the most difficult fish. It's not often that the chance comes along to work at catching a difficult reservoir fish – too often they cruise out of range after refusing a couple of casts. But I remember one Sunday in September when the chance came my way. My son Shaun and I went for an after lunch session at the Eye Brook. Estimating our chances on the journey, we decided to opt for the corner of the dam.

As most Eye Brook regulars know, the dam corner in September nearly always attracts a couple or more big browns. One reason is the tight shoal of fry that seeks the refuge of the lodge balcony; another is a deep channel 50 yards long and 15 feet or more deep, running out from the corner. This funnels the browns in to the food supply. In my wicked youth, I've had some marvellous sport here, fishing far into the night.

Shaun and I stood on the lodge balcony, and the sight of a brown of 4 lb or more cruising past in the depths was encouraging. But there was little else to be seen. An angler was packing up on the dam, and despite being there since 8 am he had only a pair of pound-and-a-half browns to show us, taken on a Baby Doll. Two other anglers who'd fished all morning had had little success.

All in all, the prospects didn't look too good. Shaun opted for the proven medium-sinker and a Baby Doll – I decided to try a contrast as the area had been fished hard with lures all morning, and opted for a leaded Hare's Ear on the point, and an Olive Buzzer on the dropper. On the second cast, a brown of 1 ¼ lb took hold of the point fly. After such instant success, I fully expected another fish, but a fruitless hour soon changed my mind. Shaun was blank too, and tried a cast here and there along the dam. He came back without a trout, but with the news that a fish was rising regularly halfway down the dam.

I decided to wander down and try it with the nymph. Sure enough, in front of the steps near the centre of the dam, a fish was dimpling the surface just 8 feet from the dam wall. Keeping well back, and watching, we were able to identify a brown of 2 lb plus. In the clear water and brightish conditions we could see it rise up from the depths, take something from the top, and leisurely go down again. It was no surprise to see that it was a brown – a rainbow would have been cruising – not holding in one spot like a river fish. For two hours I covered that brown with every nymph and presentation I could think of. The fish didn't want to know.

It's always a good idea to pause and reflect on a fishing problem – so I sat on the steps and watched. What little wind there was came from the south west, and it was slowly pushing the surface water across, forming just the hint of a wind slick, and collecting the sparse available food 8 or 10 feet from the dam, where the brown rose. But rose to what? There had been just the odd late-season olive on the wing. Could the fish be taking the odd olive nymph as it stuck in the surface tension? As I pondered that possibility, I watched the fish closer. Up it came, kissed the surface almost imperceptibly, and turned down, its tail causing the swirl we had taken for the actual rise. I was ready to try for it again, and fined down my leader to 4 lb, before tying on a single size 14 Damp Dry olive.

Still sitting on the steps so as not to stand out on the skyline, I flicked the fly to land where the fish had shown. Gradually it drifted through the feeding area and I lifted it off, and recast. This time I let the fly drift in from 4 to 5 feet upwind of the fish. After a couple of minutes, as though in slow motion, I saw the fish drift up towards the fly. It came straight up, sipped it in, and turned to go down. As it did, I lifted the rod and set the hook.

That fish fought as hard as any I have ever hooked. In the end, I netted a superb hen brownie of 2 lb 10 oz, fin-perfect, with bright red spots.

158

When spooned she was full of tiny olive nymphs, each with its wing buds on the point of bursting into the hatch.

We fished on into the dark, without any further success. I'd caught neither a big fish, nor a lot of fish; but the day, and that fish, will always stay with me – which is rare, as the fishing days seem to blend into each other over the years. Some do stand out: an exceptionally good day, a big fish, or, in this case, a difficult fish, deceived and captured on the nymph.

17·DRESSINGS

For easy reference from the text the patterns are listed in alphabetical order.

BADDOW SPECIAL

A useful general purpose stick fly or cased caddis pattern that seems to work at any depth. Well worth a try when trout are on daphnia (and a handy lure if you're desperate). Used in tiny sizes on the Bristol reservoirs with great success, apparently.

Hooks: longshank 8, 10, and 12. Generally leaded.
Silk: White.
Rib: Oval silver.
Tail: Green DFM wool or floss.
Body: Peacock herl.
Hackle: White cock, two turns.

BLACK GNAT

My copy of one of Arthur Cove's deadliest little patterns. It can be fished anytime, anywhere, with confidence. This one is particularly effective when dressed short – as tiny as a size 18 body on a size 14 hook can still kill when fish are on tiny midges.

Hooks: standard shank 10, 12, or 14.
Silk: Black.
Rib: Silver wire.
Body: Black wool or floss (dressed short).
Hackle: Black cock, two turns.

BLOODWORM

A variation on my original seal's fur Red Buzzer Larva which has had two season's successful sport to its credit. The body material has a similar translucence to the natural, and obvious body segments.
Hooks: standard shank 10 or 12.
Silk: Brown.
Body: Red polygum taken slightly around the bend.

BOOBY NYMPH

A much underused method of nymphing, but deadly for those who have mastered the technique. All nymphy colours are worth a try.
Hooks: longshank 10 and 12. Standard shank worth experimenting with.
Silk: To match body colour.
Rib: Fine wire or nylon monofilament.
Tail: Hackle fibres.
Body: Seal's fur or blended fur.
'Eyes': Two polyfoam beads encased in stocking. A figure-of-eight whip separates the beads.

BP BUZZER

At present my favourite buzzer imitator, and one that increases in popularity season by season, it seems. The dressing is intended to give you a translucent multi-coloured pattern, when compared to my old standard buzzer.
Hooks: standard shank 10, 12, or 14.
Silk: Black on black version; fawn on others.
Rib: Clear polypropylene.
Abdomen: Blended fur.

Thorax: Blended fur.
Thorax case: Feather fibre – black on black; ginger on ginger; natural hen pheasant on others.
Colour ranges: Black, brown, olive, green, claret, fawn, red, and orange.

BP NYMPH

This pattern has the same colour advantage as the BP Buzzer. Dressed in my standard longshank style, it is now my best-selling non-specific nymph, ousting even the Fraser Nymph.
Hooks: longshank 10 and 12.
Silk: As for BP Buzzers.
Rib: Clear polypropylene.
Tail: On most patterns a few tips of hen pheasant tail. Black dyed on black, ginger on ginger.
Abdomen: Blended fur.
Thorax: Blended fur.
Thorax case and legs: Hen pheasant tail fibres, colours as tails.

BROWN AND GREEN NYMPH

One of the best of my longshank Seal's Fur Nymphs. Use it if the damsel is about, or if uncertain what to use in the summer on a small water. Tie it leaded or unleaded.
Hooks: longshank 8, 10, or 12.
Silk: Brown.
Rib: Clear nylon.
Tail: Olive hackle fibres.
Abdomen: A 50/50 mix of fiery brown and dark green seal's fur.
Thorax: As above.
Wingcase and legs: Cock pheasant tail fibres (tied Fraser Nymph style).

BUZZER LARVA

This seems to be one of the least-used buzzer stages, and for me one of the most effective. When fishing deep, it's always worth a try on the point.
Hooks: standard shank 10 or 12 red; 14 or smaller green.

Silk: Brown on red; fawn on green.
Body: Red polyarn or wool; pale green yarn or wool; body goes around the bend of hook.
Rib: Clear nylon monofilament.

BUZZER PUPA

A pattern that can still be fished with confidence right through the season, and at every depth.
Hooks: standard shank 10, 12, or 14 though larger and smaller sizes can be useful.
Silk: Black, brown or fawn depending on body colour.
Rib: Clear nylon monofilament.
Abdomen: Single strand of wool.
Thorax: Dyed mole to match abdomen.
Thorax cover: Feather fibre, dyed or natural, to match body.
Colour range: Black, brown, olive, green, claret, fawn, red, and orange.

CORIXA (see also Silver Corixa)

Deadly when trout are on the naturals, and a useful fly when the trout or the angler is undecided about feeding habits. Fish in the weedy areas. The pattern can be leaded or unleaded, *but* the natural is not as plump and large as many of the so-called imitations might make you think. So don't overdo the lead underbody.
Hooks: standard shank 10, 12, or 14.
Silk: Fawn.
Body: Yellow or beige floss.
Shellback and paddles: Hen pheasant tail fibres.

COVE NYMPH

An excellent buzzer pattern, and one of the best general patterns around. The Cove Nymph was invented by that great nymph angler from Wellingborough, Northamptonshire, Arthur Cove, and used at Grafham in its early days.
Hooks: standard shank and longshank sizes 8 to 14.

163

Silk: Fawn or brown.
Rib: Copper wire or clear nylon monofilament.
Abdomen: Cock pheasant tail fibres.
Thorax: Rabbit's fur, or on my later versions, dyed mole.
Thorax cover: Cock pheasant tail.
Colour range: Thoraces in all buzzer colours are useful. Yellow and orange in a sedge hatch.

DAMP DRY

A standby whenever trout show at the surface. Good as hatching buzzers, and handy when wind-blown terrestrials get onto the water. Four basic types for all situations.
Hooks: standard shank down eyed hooks 10 to 14.

BLACK

Silk: Black.
Body: Black mole.
Hackle: Black cock, longer than a standard dry fly.

OLIVE

Silk: Fawn.
Body: Olive mole.
Hackle: Olive cock, overlarge as above.

GINGER

Silk: Fawn.
Body: Medium chestnut mole.
Hackle: Red game, overlarge as above.

GREY DUSTER

Silk: Fawn.
Body: Greyish rabbit fur.
Hackle: Badger cock, overlarge as above.

EYE BROOK CADDIS

Not just for its namesake water! This representation of the cased caddis is an excellent early season standby – but worth trying any time.

Hooks: longshank 8 to 12. Generally leaded.

Silk: Brown.

Case or 'abdomen': Medium chestnut mole.

Thorax: Narrow band of pale greenish yellow floss or wool.

Legs: One turn of natural black hen.

FRASER NYMPH

By 1986 I must have taken more trout on this pattern than all the others mentioned in this book. Consequently I have the utmost confidence in it. It seems to work at any time and at any depth. It peaks when olives hatch in numbers, when my choice is a 14. It scores even though it's several times larger than the naturals. Its other great successes have come in hatches of fawn buzzers.

Hooks: longshank 10 to 14.

Silk: Fawn.

Rib: Domestic cotton, fawn coloured.

Tail and abdomen: Between 6 and 12 fibres from the hen pheasant tail, depending on hook size. Tips form tails, the rest forms the abdomen.

Thorax: Creamy beige fur blend.

Thorax case and legs: Hen pheasant tail, tied in with tips pointing to the rear, then brought over the thorax to form legs. Roughly divide the tips to slope back on each side of the thorax, then tie down and whip finish. A standard technique on many of my nymphs.

OLIVE FRASER NYMPH

A very handy alternative: the addition of olive mole thorax, and a green cotton rib seems to change the whole body colour. Otherwise as above.

GOLD RIBBED HARE'S EAR, and variants

An excellent general purpose nymph that can be used in hatches of buzzer, sedge and olives with great confidence. Nowadays I dress them

165

with a blended fur. The natural colour is as good as ever, but I now have a whole range of these patterns available.

Hooks: standard shank 10 to 14, fine wire.
Silk: To suit body colour.
Rib: Gold or silver wire (match with colour).
Body: Blended fur (natural hare mixed with seal).
Colour range: Black, brown, olive, green, claret, fawn, red, orange, and natural.

GREEN NYMPH

This is my small fishery standby, and one of the two flies I recommend to imitate the damsel nymph. Leaded or unleaded.

Hooks: longshank 8 to 12.
Silk: Brown.
Rib: Clear nylon mono.
Tail: Olive dyed hackle fibres.
Abdomen and thorax: Olive dyed seal's fur.
Thorax case and legs: Cock pheasant tail fibres (Fraser Nymph style).

HACKLED PHEASANT TAIL

A pattern that works well for me fished high in the water, especially when olives hatch. When at a loss for a dropper pattern, this should be first choice from May onwards. The washed-out ginger pattern comes into its own in the second half of the traditional season, when the olives can be paler than early season, and sedges start to hatch.

Hooks: standard shank 10 to 14, with 12 and 14 outstanding as olives.
Silk: Brown (fawn on ginger version).
Rib: Gold wire.
Body and tail: 6 to 10 cock pheasant tail fibres, the tips forming tails, the remainder the body. Number of fibres depends on hook size. (Ginger version uses bleached PT fibres.)
Hackle: Red game, blue dun, or dyed olive cock, three turns. (Ginger variant.) Carnill ginger cock.

HARE'S EAR NYMPH, longshank

A very useful bottom-grubber and point fly at almost any time. Good as an early season Alder or cased caddis; handy for picking off cruising fish.

Hooks: longshank 8 to 12. Generally leaded.

Silk: Brown.

Rib: Oval gold.

Abdomen: Well-mixed hair from hare's mask or body. I use what I call fawn blended fur.

Thorax: As above.

Thorax cover: Any dark feather fibre – my choice is the 'bad' side of a cock pheasant side tail feather.

HATCHING SEDGE

My favourite sedge pattern which sees much use from June onwards. Although I originally had the natural hatching sedge in mind, the fly works just as well deep in the water.

Hooks: standard shank 10 to 12.

Silk: Fawn.

Rib: Rayon floss; pale yellow on yellow, green, amber, and ginger; white on the cream.

Abdomen: A 50/50 mix of bleached and dyed seal's fur.

Thorax: Fawn blended fur.

Thorax case, wings, horns, legs: feather fibre from a wing quill; hen pheasant fibre on yellow, green and cream, ginger duck on the ginger; buffy beige on the amber.

Colour range: Yellow, green, amber, ginger, and cream.

INVICTA NYMPH

A top class summer nymph with the virtues of that excellent summer colour, yellow. A standby for a sedge hatch if all else fails; and a good fly when daphnia colours the water.

Hooks: longshank 8 to 12. Leaded or unleaded.

Silk: Fawn.

Rib: Oval silver.

Tail: Yellow dyed hackle fibres.

Abdomen: Yellow dyed seal's fur.
Thorax: Yellow dyed seal's fur.
Thorax case and legs: Hen pheasant tail fibres (Fraser Nymph style).

MAYFLY NYMPH

A good small fishery nymph, which many anglers regard as a standby even at waters that don't see the natural. Always leaded.
Hooks: longshank 8 to 12.
Silk: Brown.
Rib: Copper wire.
Tail: Light creamy-fawn hackle fibres.
Abdomen: Creamy-beige blended fur.
Thorax: Fawn blended fur.
Thorax cover: Hen pheasant tail fibres (Fraser Nymph style).

SEAL'S FUR NYMPH

An excellent general purpose series, with the outline of a large translucent buzzer pupa, excellent in a hatch of large buzzers fished in steady draws just sub-surface, though their size can make them effectively stand out in a hatch of smaller flies. Large range of colour patterns and the small variations are worth listing in full. Also excellent among daphnia feeders.
Hooks: longshank 10 to 12.

RED

Silk: Brown.
Rib: Clear nylon.
Abdomen and thorax: Red seal's fur.
Thorax case: Dark brown feather fibre (Buzzer Pupa style).
Also a handy buzzer larva pattern, when it can be lightly leaded.

ORANGE

Silk: Orange.
Rib: Oval gold.

Abdomen and thorax: Orange seal.
Thorax case: Mid-brown feather fibre.

BLACK

Silk: Black.
Rib: Oval silver.
Abdomen and thorax: Black seal.
Thorax case: Black feather fibre.

OLIVE

Silk: Brown or olive.
Rib: Oval gold.
Abdomen and thorax: Olive seal.
Thorax case: Brown feather fibre.

GREEN

Silk: Green or fawn.
Rib: Oval gold.
Abdomen and thorax: Insect green seal's fur.
Thorax case: Mid-brown feather fibre.

BROWN

Silk: Brown.
Rib: Oval gold.
Abdomen and thorax: Fiery brown seal.
Thorax case: Mid-brown feather fibre.

SEDGE PUPA

My old standby pattern from June onwards. It fishes well at any depth, with short 12 inch pulls. Now I use it more as a point nymph with the hatching sedge on the dropper.
Hooks: standard shank 10 to 12.

169

Silk: Fawn.
Rib: Fawn thread.
Abdomen: Blended fur mix, 50/50 bleached and dyed seal.
Thorax: Blended fawn fur.
Abdomen and thorax case: Hen·pheasant fibre on yellow, green and cream. Carnill ginger goose or duck quill on ginger; buff-beige goose or duck quill on the amber.
Colour range: Yellow, green, amber, ginger, or cream.

SHRIMP

A standard where the natural is on the menu, but also good when picking off individual cruising fish on a small water. Its rather basic dressing means that a trout may mistake it for other food items.
Hooks: standard shank 8 to 12. Generally leaded.
Silk: Fawn or orange.
Rib: Clear nylon monofilament.
Body: Seal's fur, quite chubby, and taken slightly round the hook bend.
Colour range: Olive, brown olive, or orange.
No back or shell.

SILVER CORIXA

The 'air bubble' version of my old favourite. Possibly the best of the three I use.
Hooks: standard shank 10 to 14. Generally leaded.
Silk: Fawn.
Body: Silver lurex.
Overbody: Stretched polythene, polystickle style.
Shellback and paddles: Hen pheasant tail fibres. The body should be quite slim.

SPIDERS

A very versatile pattern, one that should always be close at hand for the dropper. Varying the size and colour means that it will cover endless situations. The colours specified are not the only useful ones, and can easily be adapted to your local water.

Hooks: standard shanks 10 to 14 (though a wider range could be useful, and they can also be dressed short on the hook shank to imitate tiny spiders, midges and terrestrials).

BLACK

Silk: Black.
Rib: Silver wire.
Body: Black mole.
Hackle: Natural black hen, two turns on all versions.

BROWN

Silk: Brown.
Rib: Gold wire.
Body: Medium chestnut mole.
Hackle: Medium red game hen.

CLARET

Silk: Brown.
Rib: Silver wire.
Body: Claret mole.
Hackle: Claret dyed hen.

ORANGE

Silk: Fawn.
Rib: Gold wire.
Body: Orange mole.
Hackle: Medium red game hen.

YELLOW

Silk: Fawn.
Rib: Gold wire.
Body: Yellow mole.
Hackle: Greenwell's hen.

SUSPENDER BUZZER

One of my favourites when trout are taking the buzzer right in the surface film.

Hooks: standard shank 10 to 14, fine wire to aid floatation.
Silk: To match body – see Buzzer Pupa.
Rib: Silver wire.
Abdomen: Seal's fur or blended fur.
Head: A foam bead encased in nylon stocking.
Colour range: As for Buzzer Pupa patterns.

ZULU NYMPH

A good general pattern, leaded or unleaded. An excellent early season grubber, and the closest thing to an out-and-out lure in these lists.

Hooks: longshank 8 to 12.
Silk: Black.
Rib: Oval silver.
Tail: Bright red hackle fibres.
Abdomen and thorax: Black seal's fur.
Thorax case and legs: Black dyed hen pheasant (Fraser Nymph style).

INDEX OF FLIES

NATURALS

ARTIFICIALS

Entries followed by † can be found illustrated in the colour section between pp96 and 97.

ACKNOWLEDGEMENTS

All photographs by Steve Windsor, except for the following: pp. 79 and 83 by John Wilshaw; colour section by Peter Hilton.